Cupcake Cash

How to Make Money with a Home-Based Baking Business Selling Cakes, Cookies, and Other Baked Goods

Jenna Richards

ISBN: 978-1-60842-772-7

Suite 264
2 Toronto St.
Toronto, ON Canada
M5C 2B5

For more information on this and other books,
visit us online at MogulMomBooks.com

TABLE of CONTENTS

Introduction

Do you love being a stay at home mom, but some days wish for a little more? Want to make a little cash, feel good about yourself and contribute to your community? Are you the mom who everyone wants to bring the cookies to the party? If so, starting a home baking business can be a rewarding and fulfilling experience that can help you give back to your family, your community and everyone who eats one of your delicious treats.

Before you put on your oven mitts and start collecting cash, there are some things you need to know about owning your own business. Now, I'm not trying to scare you away, but many people try to start their own business and fail because they didn't realize exactly what was involved.

The Nitty Gritty

Before you even think about baking your first cookie, read up on these vital points regarding starting your own business:

◆ It doesn't matter how pretty your baked goods are, how good they taste, or how many of your family and friends rave that you make the "best pies" they've ever tasted. Owning a business is hard work, and your products won't sell themselves. If you think you're going to start pulling cookies out of the oven and quickly trading them for cash, you better take a few steps back and reconsider why you're even thinking about this.

◆ Unless you have everything you need on hand (and you probably don't), you're going to have to invest some money. Not as much as if you were renting a retail space, but it will come up. I know, I know, you already have mixers, spatulas and all the cake pans you need, but do you have business cards, insurance and packaging materials?

◆ Baking for a business is not the same as baking cupcakes for your first grader's class, and there will be a point when you'll never want to see another cookie, cupcake or pie again.

◆ You'll be doing more than just baking. Owning a home bakery isn't as simple as baking cookies and exchanging them for cash that you'll then use to pay your bills. There's product development, pricing, inventory and marketing to think about. And don't forget about taxes, insurance policies, hiring employees and keeping your customers happy. These are all part of any business, and while you'll eventually be able to hire some of these jobs out, in the beginning, they're all you.

◆ You will need support. From your family especially, but also your friends. There are ways to balance everything, but you'll still have to make some sacrifices, so if your family is not on board, that will spell trouble down the road.

Now that we've got that stuff out of the way, if you're still with me, it's time to get started, but don't turn your oven on yet. Instead grab a pen and a big notebook you'll use only for your bakery business. You still have some work to do.

Chapter 1

Before Turning on the Oven

Okay, so you've decided you want to go for it, and what an awesome feeling it is! There are still some details to work out before the baking can begin, but there's nothing to say you can't bake a batch of cookies to eat while you get started.

Step 1: Decide what to sell.

The first thing you need to do is figure out what you're going to sell, and this is perhaps the most important decision you'll make regarding your business. I can hear your thoughts now, something along the lines of "I'll just sell everything." While that's ambitious, it makes things harder for several reasons:

- It makes inventory and product control almost impossible, especially since you are doing this out of your home. You probably don't have the space to store every ingredient for every item you can make, and as soon as you start getting a lot of orders, you'll learn that the more you offer, the more people want, and the more frazzled you are.

- It doesn't single you out as a baker. If you want to be known as having the "best cookies" in town, you've got to be known for cookies. Making cupcakes, pies and breads in addition to cookies, makes your customers choices much wider; too wide in fact. You need to have a specialty item.

- In the case of baking, you don't want to be a jack-of-all-trades. You want to be a master of one. There are plenty of mediocre bakeries out there with no specialty that will make whatever you want, but if nothing they make stands out, why does anyone want to go there?

I know this may be hard to grasp. After all, aren't more choices better? Aren't you limiting your customer base by not selling everything everyone wants? No and no.

Remember, you have a lot of competition. Not only from retail bakeries, but also from others just like you. You have to stand out, and the way to do that is to be known for a specialty item that people can't get anywhere else. Before you start to panic, you don't have to only make one thing; instead you should stay in the same general area. For example, if you are selling pies, you can also sell turnovers and tarts, and if you're selling cakes, you can also do cupcakes. What you want to avoid is selling a large variety of items that require vastly different ingredients, equipment and preparation methods.

How do you find that specialty item? There are some questions you should ask yourself before you just pick the first thing that comes to mind. Grab a pen and paper, and make some notes while you answer the following questions. There are five main points to consider when choosing your item, and you have to balance them all when deciding upon your niche.

1. Your product should taste amazing.

Is there something that you are known for in your circle of friends and family? Maybe everyone always asks you to bring your apple pie to parties, or you have amazing cake decorating skills. Of course, if you only make one thing for events, this question is irrelevant.

Your item should taste delicious, but different. Like there's a secret ingredient the customer just can't quite figure out.

2. Your product should stand out.

This doesn't mean that you have to use weird ingredients, or something that no one in town sells. It simply means that your product should have at least one characteristic that makes it memorable. It doesn't necessarily even have to be about the taste of the item, it can be that it's a unique shape, or has a certain appearance or packaging that stands out. Think about common baked goods and try to add your own flair to them. For example:

- Finely decorate sugar cookies with great detail

- Add course salt to the top of your chocolate chip cookies for an extra special flavor

- Make pie crusts with something other than traditional pie dough; cookie dough, for example

Whatever it is that you do, you're trying to create a perception that you are different from everyone else. Of course, you want to make sure that your product still tastes amazing,otherwise you'll be known as that weird place that makes garlic pound cake.

3. You must LOVE to bake your product.

Perhaps the most important question to be asked is, *What is it that you like to bake*? Is icing cupcakes therapeutic for you? Can you get lost in your thoughts while kneading loaves of bread? If everyone loves your pies, but you absolutely loathe rolling out pie dough, choosing pies as your specialty will get old fast. Remember, you're going to be doing this as a job, and probably for more hours than seems reasonable in the beginning; you don't want to be tired of your business before it even gets off the ground.

4. It must be cost effective.

Another thing to consider when choosing your specialty is food costs. While you don't have to think about pricing right at this minute, it helps to do some rough estimates of costs vs. what you can sell them for. For example, a loaf of bread that has only flour, salt, yeast and water will cost you pennies to make, while cookies made with expensive chocolate, butter, eggs and vanilla will cost more. Keep in mind that people tend to perceive bread as being hard to make, while cookies are something that many people will make at home, so you can probably price the bread higher, meaning you'll make more profit off a loaf of bread. This is just a quick estimate and doesn't take into consideration time, skill or whether the bread is marketable in your area, but it is something you should think about.

5. It should sell well in your area.

Now, ask yourself about the area in which you will sell your products. If you live in a small town where the $.50 donuts at the grocery store are a splurge, you're probably not going to sell a $4 cupcake. Take a look at what local bakeries in your area are selling, and what is most popular. You don't want to copy something, but just take a look at what people are buying in your area to get an idea of what you can sell. This can be hard to figure out, and the wrong decision can be costly. Asking yourself the following questions can help you figure it out:

- ◆ How many retail bakeries are in your area?

- ◆ What do they sell?

- ◆ Are prices pretty competitive, or are they all across the board?

- ◆ What is the main demographic in your community? Is it families with small children or senior citizens? Do you have a university full of college kids in your area?

In addition, you should try to determine if there is a specific niche in the area that you could fill. Is there a popular trend that hasn't yet hit your area that you can be the first baker to fill? Think along the lines of specialty products like gluten-free or vegan baked goods, or pies and tarts made only with local products. If you can come up with a product that no one else sells in your area, and do it well, then the advantage of being the first one to do it can put you well ahead of your competition.

Of course, you also have to keep in mind that it's possible that the reason there isn't already someone selling in a particular niche is because there isn't a need or market for one in your community. A small farming town out in the country probably doesn't have enough vegans to support a vegan bakery, but a metropolitan area with a campus full of college students may be the perfect spot to market your vegan products.

There are several ways that you can find out what might work without purely guessing, although at some point you may just have to take a risk and hope for the best. You'll never know until you try. In the meantime, try the following:

- Visit local farmers markets in your area and see what kinds of products they sell. You can also talk to the vendors to see if you can get some insight, although you probably shouldn't mention that you're thinking of starting a bakery; this is your competition after all.

- Visit local bakeries in your area, see what they sell and ask what their most popular items are. Buy a few things here and there; taste them and ask yourself how you can improve on them.

- Use the power of Google. You can find out a lot of information simply by doing some online searches. Search for things such as bakeries in your area, and read reviews on sites such as Yelp. Pay particular attention to what products people love and hate. You may be surprised to find all sorts of niches are already filled, and that you don't know of every single bakery in town. Look for home bakers as well; most will probably have at least a website telling you what they sell, how to purchase from them, and what their specialty is. Also search for food and bakery trends in general. It's a good idea to invest several hours of just reading through all the information you can find before settling on anything; not only will you find information on what you're looking for, you'll also probably find inspiration you otherwise would have missed.

- Visit local gourmet food stores and see what they are selling. Pay particular interest if they have a section dedicated to local retailers. Look at what they are selling and do your best to determine how long something has been sitting on a shelf. Are the cookies hard? They may not be big sellers in that case. Talk to a store manager and tell him your plans to get information about possibly putting items in the store. Not only is this a great idea for the future, but also he'll probably tell you information such as what sells and what doesn't; they don't want products sitting on the shelf longer than they have to.

- Ask around. Next time you're at a PTA meeting, ask other parents what bakeries and products they like. Talk to your neighbors, friends and family members about what they currently purchase and what they think is missing. Be sure to ask as many people as you can, from as many age groups, social groups and ethnicities as possible to get a wide variety of opinions.

- Next time you're dining out in a local restaurant, look at the dessert menu. Ask your server what the most popular item is and if they get any special requests. Also ask if they make their desserts in house, or where they get them. Do this in several restaurants all over town.

Now that you've got more insight on what may be the best thing to sell, you just have to come up with the right item. It's a lot of information to take in all at once, and a decision that you shouldn't take lightly. To summarize, when choosing an item to be your specialty, you want something that:

- Tastes delicious, but stands out
- You love to bake

- Is cost effective and profitable
- Will sell in your area

Take your time, make pro and con lists, and talk it over with your loved ones. This isn't something that you'll be able to change (at least not very easily), so you want to make sure that you find the perfect product. You can always change or add to your menu in the future, but to get started you'll have to really wow people right off the bat.

Let's say for my at-home bakery I'm going to make brownies. I'll use this as an example in the book. Let me tell you a bit about my brownies.

- They're going to be round instead of square

- They'll be available in a variety of flavors

- They'll be visually stunning (to go with the round shape); hand decorated

- They'll be all natural, made with the highest-quality ingredients

Defining Your Products

After you've chosen what you're going to sell, the next step is to analyze it, and determine exactly what it is you are offering and to whom. This will help your customers differentiate you from your competitors.

There are four factors we're going to talk about when it comes to defining your products:

- Price

- Characteristics

- How it's used

- What problem it solves

Price

This is probably the easiest way for your customers to differentiate between you and your competitor, because it's one that's spelled out clearly and is easy to understand. If you're selling cookies for a dollar, and the bakery down the street sells them for two, you have an advantage. Just be careful when using this positioning strategy, as you don't want to be known only because you sell cheap baked goods. (You probably don't want to have the highest prices in town either.)

Because I want my brownies to be made from high-quality ingredients I may have to price them higher, but because they don't come from a boxed mix, I think my customers will think they are worth it.

Characteristics

This is where you determine what your product has that another does not. Maybe your angle is that you use only natural products, or seasonal ingredients, or maybe it's that your cakes are made by hand from scratch, while the local bakery in town uses a mix.

For my brownie business, I'm offering brownies in several flavors, and the round shape and visually appealing look will be a perfect combination of elegant and familiar.

How Your Product is Used

Are you making desserts that people will want to take to fancy dinner parties? Scones and breakfast pastries that are perfect for early morning meetings? Or maybe you're making artisan bread that is the perfect complement to a rustic meal. Whatever it is, makes sure that your product has a *purpose* that will help people understand why they need it.

My brownies are a great alternative to cupcakes and cookies at parties, and a great choice for picnics and other places where you want a delicious, easy-to-eat treat.

What Problem it Solves

You may be wondering how baked goods can solve any problems (or you may not), but hear me out. If you have a child who has gluten intolerance, a gluten-free cookie can be a lifesaver. Or maybe you make healthy products that are perfect for those trying to watch their weight. The point is, whatever it may be, if your products can be the solution to a problem your customers have, they are more likely to buy it.

Do my brownies really solve a problem? Well, I can market them as a great corporate gift, or an alternative to cupcakes and cookies for parties.

Step 2: Test your recipes.

Now we're starting to get into the fun part of the business; we're going to test your recipes. You may be thinking that you've already got your recipes down pat, and you can skip this part, but you're wrong. Testing your recipes will save you time, money and hassle in the long run. This is a time consuming process and may require lots of time in the kitchen, so put your apron on, and let's get started.

Your goal is to end up with recipes that are easy to follow, cost effective and turn out products that are consistent in both flavor and size every single time. When you're through with the long and exhausting testing process (yes, you will be tired), you should have a recipe binder with all of your recipes laid out in detail. Eventually you'll probably need some help, and when that time comes, you should just be able to hand over your book with little to no explanation.

Before you begin, you need to do the following:

◆ Lay out any recipes for products that you are going to use. Most recipes you'll find in cookbooks and online are home baking recipes, which differ greatly from commercial recipes. You're going to have to do your best to convert them by changing measurements, ingredients and production methods to those that save time and money.

◆ Look over the ingredients. You'll probably see a lot of the same things: Flour, sugar, butter, eggs, etc., but what about ingredients like chocolate, nuts or extracts? These are all things you may want to find substitutes for, mostly due to cost, and this is where the testing process comes in handy. Maybe you make the best chocolate cake in the world, but you use expensive imported chocolate. This is fine for a family dinner, but if you're going to sell that same cake over and over, you either have to find a worthy substitute, or pass that cost on to the customer. Keep in mind when choosing ingredients that you should pick those that are fairly easy to source, but also easy to replace in case you can't get that particular product for some reason.

◆ You'll need to test everything. Don't assume that you can swap store brand flour for the expensive name brand with the same results, and the same goes for everything else. When buying ingredients for the testing process, get several types of everything, being sure to note the cost.

◆ Because your goal is consistency, you'll need to rethink the way you measure. If you currently measure flour with a measuring cup or vanilla by simply pouring a splash in your cake batter, you're costing yourself both money and consistency, two things that can ruin a business before it's started. The first thing you need is a bakers scale. There are several types out there; most commercial bakeries use balance scales, but a small digital or spring scale will work in the beginning. Next, you're going to have to decide on sizes for your products, and get scoops and measuring cups to match. You don't want to have to eyeball anything, so make sure if you're going to scoop a half cup of cupcake batter into a pan, that you get half cup scoops.

◆ You'll need to determine the conversions for scooping vs. weighing things like flour and sugar. A cup of flour is about 4 ounces, but depending on how you measure, you could be using 5 or 6 ounces of flour in your recipe. Make your recipe exactly as you normally would using measuring cups, but before adding an ingredient to your bowl, weight it and write it down.

When testing:

Grab a pen and paper, and write everything down each time. Write down:

- The brands you use

- Exact measurements

- Oven and stove temperatures

- Baking times

- Baking pans you've used

In a commercial kitchen, everything is pretty standard, but in your home kitchen, you probably have different sizes and weights of pans, casserole dishes, and other equipment. There's no need to run out and buy new, but you do have to know what kind of result you get with each one to avoid a product turning out differently and you left standing there with your mouth open wondering why.

Taste each product when it's cool and put some of each batch aside so that you can compare. Ask your family members to taste with you, and make notes on each recipe. Maybe that high quality chocolate makes a huge difference to you; but your customers aren't going to pay an extra dollar per cupcake. Only you can really decide that, but you don't know unless you test.

A fun way to get feedback is to have a tasting party. Invite friends and family over for a tasting session after you've cleaned everything up, and let them tell you what they think. Make sure you have several samples of all of your items on hand, and that you know which is which. You can give each item a number, and ask your tasters to fill out a questionnaire based on each one. Don't make it long or boring, just enough to judge which one is best. Don't let anyone know which is which, you want honest and unbiased feedback, and be sure to tell your guests to let you know if they absolutely do not like something; you don't want to waste your time trying to sell a product that won't sell.

Once your guests have left, look over their responses, and tally up which items got the most positive feedback. Maybe vanilla beans sourced from Uganda that you have to buy 50 pounds of at a time are worth it, maybe they're not; you'll never know until you try.

Step 3: Name your products.

Once you have decided which recipes are going to be your stars, you need to get them named and organized. Yes, named. Were you just going to put Chocolate Cake on your menu? You can do that if you want, but a more creative and fun way to put them on your menu is by coming up with names that make them stand out. Everyone makes chocolate cake, but not everyone makes Betsy's Super Delicious Dark Chocolate Cake With Super Creamy Buttercream Icing. Remember, you are trying to stand out here, not blend in with the crowd.

Tips for naming your baked goods:

- You want the name you choose for each product to clearly define what it is, but also be descriptive and appealing.

- Keep it short if you can.

- Remember, you're trying to sell the product, and often times the name alone can do that. Caramelized Banana Brownies with Peanut Buttery Buttercream sound better than Banana Brownie with Peanut Butter Icing. Don't lie in the name, but use appetizing ingredients or cooking preparations to their full advantage. Which would you rather have Vanilla Bean Cheesecake or Vanilla Cheesecake? It's the same product, but that one word makes it seem more upscale and thus, more delicious.

- Look at menus for other bakeries, but only use them for inspiration; don't copy anything word for word.

Step 4: Package your products.

So you've got a product to sell, perfected your recipes and given them creative names. Now what?

Well now you need to think about how you're going to package them. You weren't going to just hand your baked goods over on your pans, plates or containers, were you? That could get costly. You'll need boxes, bags, labels and more depending on what you're selling.

There are a couple ways you can go when packaging. For my brownie business, I'm going to market my brownies as great gifts, so packaging is important. This will also add to the cost of the brownies, but my thinking is that people will spend more money on a gift than they will just an everyday snack, so they'll pay the higher price.

Your goal is to find packaging that fits your budget and your products, as well as who you're trying to sell to. There are many, many options from plain white boxes that are available at your restaurant supply store to beautiful boxes that are embossed with your logo. You'll also need to think about labels. Not only to avoid a mix-up when you're selling at a farmer's market or other location, but also because you want people to remember you, and if they pull a bagged cookie without a label from their purse, they may *ooh* and *ahh* over how good it tastes, but have no way to know how to get another one.

When it comes to packaging, you need to keep cost in mind, and if it is something that adds to your overall appeal, you may need to factor that in your price. Don't go too crazy though; no matter how pretty your packaging is, it will most likely always get thrown away.

Okay, so now we've got great recipes for amazing products with fun names that are packaged well. Keep reading to learn how to set up your business.

Chapter 2

Setting Up Your Business

Now that you know what you're going to sell, we're almost ready to start baking, but there are still a few things you have to do.

I know you're ready to start baking, but if you want to have a profitable business that will support you and your family for years to come you have to lay a proper foundation, and that's what we're going to do now. In this chapter, you're going to get your business set up, and we're going to break it down in a few easy steps:

1. Creating a vision

2. Create a business plan

3. Get licensed in your state

4. Learn the health code regulations in your state

5. Get your kitchen organized and create a schedule

So, if you're ready to get started, grab your notebook and a pen, and let's get through this stuff so you can finally turn that oven on.

Step 1: Create your vision.

Yes, you've decided what you're going to sell, and maybe even to whom you're going to sell, but this step is more that that. This step is about figuring out exactly what you want to get out of your business. So grab your notebook and write down the answers to the following questions. Don't rush it, and be honest about what you want. You're doing this for you and you only, so guessing what the right answers are will get you nowhere. There are no right answers!

- Why do you want to open your own business?

- What is your goal for your business? Do you want to simply be a small local bakery that always makes everything by hand, or do you have visions of factories and multiple locations? What do you want to be known for?

- Where do you see yourself in one year? Five years? Ten?

- Are you going into business solely to make money or are you doing it for your love of baking?

- How much money do you want or have to invest in your business upfront? This can be a difficult question, but one you should seriously take the time to answer before getting started. Are you willing to start out taking out small business loans? They'll give you a head start and get you on the fast track a bit faster, but you'll have to pay these back even if your business is not successful.

- Do you see yourself continuing your business after it is financially successful, or would you consider selling?

If you don't know the answers to these questions, that's okay. After all, you can't really decide right now if you would sell your business down the road; you have no idea where life will take you. The whole point of this exercise is just to get some ideas and get you considering your options. Nothing you say here is set in stone, and remember, no one has to see this unless you want them to. So take your time and think about these answers. Come back to them if you have new ideas. If you've never been in business before, you can't possibly know the challenges and ideas that will come up, so while you shouldn't take this exercise too seriously, you should not skip it either.

Step 2: Create a business plan.

Part of the appeal of starting a home-based bakery business instead of trying to start a commercial business is that you hopefully won't need to secure funds, at least at first. After all, much of what you would need funding for in a commercial business – such as ovens and other tools – you probably already have in your house. You don't know, however, that you won't want to open a commercial space someday, and for this reason, it's a good idea to create a business plan now. Of course, if you do need or want to get a business loan, you will need a business plan. That's up to you however. If you're unsure about whether you need a loan, refer to your notes about creating a vision, talk it over with family members if necessary, but don't take the financial aspect of owning a business lightly. While you won't have a lot of overhead, there is still no guarantee that you will make a profit in the first year or two.

In addition to helping you secure funding now or in the future, a business plan can be a helpful tool in establishing your vision, helping you think about things you may overlook, and keeping tabs on your progress over the years. It's not that difficult to create, and you'll be surprised at how helpful just the process of doing it is.

To secure loans and other funding, you'll need a formal business plan. A formal business plan is best created with the help of a lawyer or financial advisor, so we're going to simply create a modified business plan. For more information on writing a formal business plan, go to sba.gov. You'll find all kinds of helpful information there, including professionals to help you, and secure funds through methods other than loans.

The good news is that if you've gone through all the steps in Chapter 1 about researching your product and it's marketability in your area, this should be a fairly quick process, but you should still take your time, and do it correctly. So grab your notebook, and let's get started. You can make an outline in your business notebook and then transfer the information to the computer, or you can go right to the computer if you'd like. I prefer to have all of my information in one place at first, so I prefer the extra step of writing it down, but if you'd like to skip that step, feel free.

> **Tip:** When writing your modified plan, write it as though you are asking someone for money. Keep it positive, and do your best to sell yourself and convince whoever is reading it (which may be no one at the moment) that you are a good investment.

Executive Summary:

This is basically just a summary of what your business is about. What are you selling? Who are you selling it to? It doesn't have to be long, it just has to give someone an idea of who you are and what your business is about.

Company Description:

Similar to an Executive Summary, you're going to write a description of your company. Include the name of your business (if you don't have one, we'll go over that in the next section), the year you're starting, and a brief description. Usually this would include how much money you've made, but since you're starting out, you don't have to worry about that.

Product or Service: Be brief, but focus on why a customer wants what you're selling.

Market Analysis:

Describe the market you are selling to, your customer demographics and needs, and how you're going to market to them.

Strategy and Implementation:

This can be tough not having started, but this is an overall description of how you will manage your business. You want to describe the way you're going to track results. You can write down what you know, and come back to this later after you have a better idea if you'd like.

Financial Analysis:

This is something else that you probably won't really know until you've been at it for at least six months. This is where you would put projected profit and loss reports, and anything else related to finances and cash flow.

Management Team:

This is where you'll list your employees and what their part in your organization is. If it's just you for now, this simply means listing everything you're doing to get the business going, and how you are going to keep in operating on a day-to-day basis.

These aren't the only things you can include in your business plan, but this will get you started. Remember, if you're going to try to get loans or other funding, you'll need a formal business plan, and for that you will definitely need professional advice.

Step 3: Get licensed in your state.

This step is actually easier than most people think, but there are some things to take into consideration because you will be selling food.

First you'll need to get your name registered. If you don't have a name for your business, this is a good time to create one, since now you'll have to register it in your state. Here are some tips for naming your business:

◆ Keep it simple. You don't want something too long for people to remember.

- Keep your vision in mind when choosing a name. If you're goal is to eventually have a giant corporation, naming your business "Barbara's Home-style Bakery" could be misleading down the road.

- If possible, you should name your business something that instantly conveys what it is you're doing. "Abby's Cookie Creations" is better than "Abby's Creations."

- Be creative, but try to avoid intentional misspellings to be cute such as "Kandy's Kakes" for example. This can be a turn off to some people, creating the wrong image, and in addition it can create problems for people looking for you online or in a phone book. If someone recommends you by word of mouth, a customer may try different spellings of "candy," but probably not "cake."

- Do your best to stand out, but don't be too out there.

Remember, your name should reflect who you are and what your business is.

If you haven't decided on a name, it's best to do so while you're getting your license so you can check things as you go. Most states have a directory where you can search business names that others are using.

Now that you have a name, you're next step is to get registered. The laws are different in every state, but you'll need to get a tax ID number and possibly a vendor's license. You can probably do all of these things online, pay the registry fees, and they'll mail you a license.

Tip: Avoid websites that charge you a processing fee for services such as getting a Tax ID number. You have to pay the license fees regardless, and these sites will charge you hundreds of dollars on top of that to do something you can easily do yourself. Irs.gov has many resources for small business owners, so you should start there before looking at a site you found at the top of a Google search. Once you have your corporation set up, you can now use it to open a business bank account, apply for a vendor's license and get registered with your local health department, which is the next step you're going to take.

Step 4: Register with your local health department.

If you are going to be selling food, whether out of your house or in a commercial space, you MUST contact your local health department to see what you'll need to do to keep everything on the up and up. In some states, the laws are pretty relaxed as far as selling food items out of your home; in others it is against the law, in which case you'll need to alter your plans. What you do not want to do is start selling without checking only to get shut down – or worse – down the road.

Like getting your business license, the health department laws vary from state to state, so you won't find exactly what you need to do here, but I'll give you a general idea.

Before you contact the health department, you'll need to tell them what you're selling, and probably be prepared for a visit and inspection. In some cases, modifications may need to be made in order to ensure that your kitchen is safe for selling food products to the public.

There are no laws about how you must keep your kitchen in order to feed your family, but for public consumption, you will have to rethink the way you prepare foods, the way you store your inventory, and how clean you keep your kitchen. You also have to keep in mind that just as a restaurant may be subject to a surprise inspection, you may be too, so you'll want to set some "business hours," (i.e. the hours when you will be baking for your business). You can still use your kitchen for your business any time of day, but this way you are limiting the times in which a surprise inspection can occur.

The health department can tell you the next step you'll need to take and provide literature or resources on how you can get your kitchen up to speed. Depending on where you live, there could be zoning issues, equipment issues and storage concerns. You may have to store your business foods separate from your personal foods, which could pose a problem with things like refrigeration. It should go without saying that before you have a health inspector visit your home, clean it until it is spotless. This means making sure cabinets and drawers are free of crumbs, and that your refrigerator is cleaned out and only contains fresh foods. Pull all of your appliances out and vacuum the floors. You don't want to give a health inspector any reason to not allow you to sell your products from your home. While they will tell you how to get your kitchen up to speed, if it is not clean, they could shut you down before you start. So start cleaning.

Other things you need to consider when it comes to health regulations:

- Do you have pets? You'll have to be able to clearly demonstrate to the health department how you will keep them out of your kitchen.

- You'll need to rearrange your kitchen to assure that food is stored properly, and kept away from chemicals, such as cleaning products.

- You'll need to arrange your refrigerator so that it meets health department standards.

- Keep in mind that while you may cook in your bare feet or with your hair down for your family, you may not be able to do so when in business.

These aren't your only concerns of course. The only thing you can surely control right now is that your kitchen is spotlessly clean. For more information on safety and sanitation for food service businesses, go to www.servsafe.com. You'll find great resources, as well as information about obtaining a certification that meets industry standards.

What happens if I can't sell baked goods out of my home?

Besides the fact that you may not be able to sell food out of your home in your state, there are other reasons you may have been stopped here. Maybe the zoning requirements are just too expensive, or your kitchen isn't big enough. Whatever the reason, you don't have to give up just yet.

While this is a major setback, it doesn't have to be the end of your business. You have a couple options that don't require leases and buying expensive equipment.

First, do some searches to find out if there are any commercial bakeries for rent in your area. Also known as "incubator kitchens," these are professional kitchens that are set up specifically for people like you who – for whatever reason – can't use their home kitchen. These are usually fully equipped with professional equipment and you rent them by the hour. They are mostly used by caterers, but are perfect in this situation. There are definite pros and cons to these, and you may find them worth looking into even if you do have a set up that will allow you to bake at home. For starters, you won't be wearing out your home oven and other equipment, and you'll probably be able to get more done in a shorter amount of time due to larger ovens and more counter space. The downside is that you won't be able to bake whenever you feel like it, you'll have to get on a schedule to assure you always have time to bake, and you'll have to come up with a solution to bring your ingredients back and forth, as these aren't usually included. Either way, this is a great option that is a good middle ground between baking in your home kitchen and starting from scratch in commercial space.

Another option is to contact smaller local bakeries in your area and see about renting their space from them during their off hours. This can be hit or miss, as many will immediately say no, but if you find a small bakery that may be struggling financially, they may be interested in working out some kind of arrangement. Many small places are closed one day a week such as Sundays, so you may be able to rent one day a week for a reasonable price. You also might be able to work out an agreement as far as supplies go, so that you can use their products and pay them instead of having to lug your own stuff around. You can work out the details with the owner of the bakery, but this can be an option that can work out nicely for all parties if you can find someone who will rent to you for a reasonable rate.

Whatever you decide to do, it is worth repeating that you do NOT want to skip the part of contacting the health department. They can and will shut you down if you don't follow the rules in your local area.

Step 5: Organize your kitchen and create a schedule.

Getting Organized

Once you've contacted your health department and gotten the OK to bake out of your kitchen, the next step is to get it set up for your business.

I'm not going to lie, this will be a huge pain in the you-know-what, but it is a necessary step to ensure organization, and will help keep your business on track. There are several reasons you'll want to do this, including:

- To keep up to health department standards. While they may not require specifics, some things are always a good idea, such as keeping food separated from cleaning supplies, and storing food properly. Remember, you are not only risking your family's safety at this point, you are now putting everyone who eats your products at risk. Hopefully that will be a lot of people, and the last thing you want is to make someone sick.

- You'll want to separate your household groceries from your business. You don't want your family using business products without your knowledge only to run out when you need it.

- You'll need to have a system set up to keep inventory, which will in turn help keep food costs down.

So where do you start? Well, before you start tearing up your kitchen, you need to take a look at the recipes for everything you'll be selling on a regular basis and make a list of products that you will always have to keep on hand. If you're starting with a small number of products, this list should be fairly short.

- Before you think about where you're going to store all this stuff, you need to think about how much you'll need. This can be difficult to gauge at first, but you can be pretty sure that even just selling a moderate amount, you'll be using a lot of flour and sugar. It probably won't be cost effective to buy the five-pound bags you usually buy, which means you may be buying 20-pound bags or larger. That's not going to fit in your cupboard, so where you going to put it? You'll probably have to buy storage bins that won't fit in your cabinets, which means that you'll need to have a spot to put them in the kitchen where they won't be in your way. This may mean moving stuff around, and this may take some time to figure out.

- For products that you will always need but can keep smaller quantities of, such as chocolate, baking powder and such, you'll need to dedicate a cabinet space only for business items. If you find yourself short on space, this may be difficult to get used to and will probably require an adjustment to your family grocery and kitchen habits. You will want to let everyone in the house know that that cabinet is off limits, and you'll need to get in the habit of always putting business products away in the designated areas.

- You will also need to section off a small section of your refrigerator and probably your freezer, unless you have a spare you can set up in a garage or basement. Again, everyone in the house needs to know what they can use and can't. You will probably have to purchase separate eggs, butter, and milk for the home and business. It's inconvenient, but once you get used to it, you won't even think about it anymore.

- You need to make sure that everything, including items that will be used for the household, is stored up to health department standards too. This means that even though you may not be using meat or veggies for your business, they'll need to be stored in the proper place in your refrigerator. During a health inspection, they will be inspecting the entire kitchen, so it needs to all be up to code.

Creating a Schedule

Getting a schedule down will be difficult in the beginning, but you need to make sure you are prepared. Keep in mind that unless you hire employees, you will be doing everything yourself, and this is way more than just baking. In addition to creating products, you will need to handle banking and finances, taxes, marketing, inventory, and website and order management. You'll be dealing with customers, and scheduling pickups and drop offs of products. You have to have some kind of schedule to manage all of these things. Some tips:

- Grab a calendar or your notebook, and take a look at what you've already got going on that you can't change. This could be kids' events, family commitments, or driving kids to and from school. You'll have to work around these.

- Designate specific times to do specific things. Some things, such as marketing, may only require a few hours a week, while other things such as managing orders will require daily maintenance. Have set times that you do these things. For example, maybe you handle orders for one hour everyday after you drop the kids of at school, and you bake three days a week at set times. Put them on your calendar.

- Try to be as specific as possible about times. For example, instead of listing your Monday as: Managing orders, shopping and baking, list it as: Managing orders from 9 a.m. to 10 a.m., shopping from 11 a.m. to 1 p.m. and baking from 2 p.m. to 6 p.m. It can take some time to figure out just how long certain things will take, but if you have set times for tasks, you are much less likely to fall victim of procrastination and rushing to get things done in time.

- Combine household chores with business obligations if you can. For example, you can probably do your household grocery shopping and business shopping at the same time. Just be sure to pay for everything separately.

- It's better to do a weekly or biweekly schedule to keep up with the flow of business. Some things, such as recipe testing or taxes, may not need to be done every week, but you'll need to have time to do them when they need to get done.

- You'll need to set up some kind of schedule for your customers so that you aren't always doing impromptu baking when you don't have time. If you bake on Monday, Wednesday and Friday for example, you can schedule pick-ups for Tuesday, Thursday and Saturday. Ideally you'll want your customers to place orders and plan in advance; you're only one person after all, not a 24-hour mega supermarket. Whatever your schedule is, you want to make sure that you know it and your customers know it. You can add a surcharge for rush orders if you'd like, but be prepared to fit all of those in if you promise them. Sometimes, all the money in the world isn't going to make you want to bake more cookies during your rare moments of spare time.

- Get in the habit of sticking to your schedule. This may be hard at first, but it's important not to get behind. There are several nice things about working from your house and one of those is being able to set your own schedule. The downside is that it can be very hard to keep it if you don't have anyone holding you accountable every day. Remember, if you want to succeed, you have to be accountable for yourself. It can be nice to sleep in an extra hour here and there, but if you do that too often, your business will suffer.

- While you will be working a lot of hours when you first start, you need to schedule some time off, preferably one full day a week that you can spend with your family, then maybe a couple hours a day, making sure to make time for yourself. Put these on the calendar, and do your very best to not cut into that time with business related tasks.

- The best way to avoid cutting into personal time is to work when you schedule yourself to work. Yes, doing your weekly books can be boring, but if you schedule yourself to do it from 10 a.m. to 12 p.m., then do it during that time or until it is done. If you have time leftover that's great, but don't get behind because you're procrastinating. Remember, you are working for yourself now, so when you don't get something done, you are the one who suffers either by having to work on your day off, or not making enough money to keep the business going.

- Keep your family in the loop about your schedule. Make sure that if you are in the kitchen baking, they know it is off limits during those times. Let them know when you'll be working, but don't forget you have to make time for them too.

Does all of this sound difficult and overwhelming? In the next chapter, we'll show you how to manage it all.

Chapter 3

Product Creation

In this chapter, you should already have your basic products down, but you still have questions regarding perfecting your recipes, creating a production schedule that works, and figuring out how much to make.

We went over a little bit of this stuff in Chapter 2, so you shouldn't have too much trouble, but now we're going to make sure everything is perfect so that you can start baking, selling and collecting money so that all your hard work will finally pay off!

Setting Policies and Procedures

Policies and procedures are for both your benefit and your customers'. They ensure consistency, customer satisfaction and organization. Once you've set some policies and procedures, you should write them up in easy to understand language and post them on your website or any printed items that you want to give out. Try not to make them too long; include only the information your customer needs to know.

Your policies and procedures will include:

- ◆ Perfecting your recipes
- ◆ Your production schedule

- Holiday/seasonal production

- Order policy

- Your pickup/delivery schedule

- Payment types accepted

- Refund policy

- Freshness and storage of your products

- How much should I make?

- Customer feedback

Perfecting Your Recipes

By now, you should have decided what you want to sell (in my case, I'm going to sell those round brownies I talked about), and you should have tested your recipes so that they taste great. The next step is to make sure they are sale ready. What do I mean? Well, how do they look? Do they have the same taste and texture every single time? If you're making something for a single serving, such as cookies or cupcakes, are they the same size and shape?

Remember that you're not home baking anymore; you're now a commercial baker. This means you need to work like one. If you've never been formally trained, that's OK, but your customers won't give you any slack when it comes to their expectations. They want a product that is the same every time; this is why they are ordering from a professional instead of doing it themselves.

While your family may not care if you're famous chocolate chip cookies are exactly the same at a family party, a customer will. Remember, your customer is paying for a product that they expect to be consistent every time they buy them. How do you achieve all this perfection? Follow these tips:

- Always measure everything according to your recipe. No more pinches of cinnamon or splashes of vanilla. It can be a pain, yes, but if you don't want variations, this is the only way to go.

- Use the same ingredients as often as you can. This means you want the same brand of flour, the same type of butter, and if your recipe calls for large eggs, medium won't do. When deciding on ingredients for your recipes, you want to make sure that what you are using is easy to source; it's not a bad idea to try to find a suitable substitute in case of an emergency, but this will require more recipe testing. Only use your substitution when absolutely necessary.

- For cupcakes, cookies and other small items, use measuring cups or scoops to ensure all items are the same size.

- Get a scale and weigh ingredients such as flour and sugar. You'll have a much more consistent product.

- For decorated items, the best way to get consistent products is to practice, practice, practice!

- To determine how good your products are after you've baked them, you should taste them the same day you've baked them, the next day and the day after that. This will help you determine at what point they are no longer good for sale. A good rule of thumb is that an item should not be sold more than one day after being made, but it also depends on the individual item for sale. You can only really know by testing and tasting, as some products may still be good two days later.

- Once you start baking items for your customers, it's a good idea to taste each batch to ensure they are good before they go out the door. You may not know you forgot to add salt to that batch until you've tasted it, and you certainly do not want that batch to make it to the customer.

- If a batch comes out of the oven and you feel like it's not exactly right, get rid of it even if you can't quite pinpoint what's wrong.

- Make sure that you are baking your items in the same thing you will sell them in. For example, let's say you're baking pies. It can seem like a waste to bake them in disposable tins for the testing process when you have pie pans in your kitchen, but that will change the end result. It's important that when you are perfecting your recipes for sale that you bake them exactly as you would when selling them, even if it seems wasteful or not cost effective.

Once you've perfected your recipe, you should create a binder with each of the recipes. This will ensure that if you have someone else making them, they follow the recipe exactly as you do. Put them in plastic pages, and make sure each of the recipes includes the following:

- The product name as it will be seen to the customer. Remember, it should be appealing, descriptive and fun.

- All of the ingredients in the recipe. You should list the ingredients in the order in which they will be added, and the type of ingredient and measurements should be clear. Try to spell out as much as you can, and specify container sizes when necessary (4 ounce can, 8 ounce bag).

- Be detailed with the ingredient names. Don't just say "flour" if you've got several types of flour in your kitchen; specify cake flour, all purpose flour, or whatever it is you're using.

- Make sure your instructions are detailed, and that they state the type and size of pan, oven temperature, approximate baking time, and measuring utensil used to scoop the product.

- Have a section for each recipe with notes on product substitutions etc.

- Write all recipes in the same format, and type them up so that they can easily be read. Putting them in sheet protectors keeps them from getting harmed by spills and such.

Creating a Production Schedule

Now that you've got your products down pat, it's time to create a production schedule. It will be fairly easy in the beginning, especially if it's just you, but you need to plan on hiring employees, and in that case you'll want your schedule to flow smoothly.

- First, think about the size of your kitchen. How many people will ideally fit without constantly bumping into each other? Ideally, you'll probably want to set up each person at his or her own station. Too many people in the kitchen will lead to far less efficiency.

- Timing is everything. You need to create a production schedule that results in customers getting their products when they expect them. Do not tell your customers that they will get something hot out of the oven if you simply can't do it. Instead give reasonable expectations and only make promises that you know you can keep.

- In order to create the most efficient production schedule, you need to think about when and where you're going to sell your products. If you're going to sell at a farmer's market on Saturday, you'll have to spend all day on Friday baking. You'll also need to think about whether you're going to have customers pick up at your house, and when. You can also take special orders to have ready at the farmer's market.

- Remember that your family must use the kitchen too, so you'll need to plan around their schedule. If your kids are in school, and your husband works during the day, this is the best time to use the kitchen, at least for the bulk of your production. You may overlap slightly; you'll just have to make sure your family knows they have to stay out of the kitchen as much as possible.

- Instead of baking everything every time you're in the kitchen, you should bake different things on different days. For example, maybe Monday will be the day you do chocolate products,

Tuesday you'll do vanilla, and Wednesday you'll do decorated. Once you create a menu, you can share it with your customers on your website, or print it out and hand it out at the farmer's market. Your customers will get used to the idea that you don't have everything every day, and will place orders for what they want when you have it. This method will make everything much easier, especially if your kitchen is small.

- If you must bake different products for different events on the same day, organize them so that the items that will last longer are baked first. For example, quick breads and pound cakes will usually last a day or two, but you generally want to eat cookies as soon as possible after they've come out of the oven. In this case, you should bake your quick breads first and your cookies last.

- Set up stations in your kitchen, kind of like an assembly line. Set up a mixing area where you will mix your batters and dough, followed by an area where everything gets panned up, and finally, a place where everything goes to cool. This will help you avoid chaos and confusion, especially when you have people helping you out. Make sure that the set up makes sense. You wouldn't want your mixing station to be set up next to the oven, while your cooling station is set up across the room. Use common sense when setting up your assembly line, and then stick to it every time you bake.

- Remember that you have to include packaging in your production schedule. A good way to handle this is to do it after you're done baking. Clean your kitchen, and then set up a packaging station.

- Set up a small whiteboard in your kitchen that will have your production schedule for the day on it. You can list special orders in the order they need to be baked; that way you can just get in the kitchen and get started, checking off the items as you go.

Holiday Production

The holidays are probably going to be your busiest times of the year, so you need to really plan ahead and try to keep as organized as possible, especially the first year you're in business. You'll need to incorporate a holiday production schedule into your regular baking schedule. This may mean cutting back on some things during the busy season.

You'll more than likely have to change your products with the seasons, so you'll have to account for testing new recipes, as well as fitting them into your production schedule. You should plan in advance to have something special for the following holidays:

- Valentine's Day

- Easter

- 4th of July

- Halloween

- Thanksgiving

- Christmas

These are holidays that people tend to buy more baked goods to take to cookouts, parties, etc. It doesn't have to be anything fancy or special; it can be the same sugar cookies you make every day with different colored icing or sprinkles, especially for minor holidays such as 4th of July. For bigger holidays, you may want to have totally different items.

You also need to plan way in advance when it comes to holiday baking. I would recommend thinking about holiday items at least a month in advance for everything except for Christmas; you should plan at least two months in advance. You'll have to include recipe creation, product testing, and advertising, as well as everything else that goes into selling new products.

You'll also need to think about when you're going to sell something for a specific holiday. You can probably get away with selling Valentine's Day items for only a week before the holiday, whereas for Christmas items, you'll probably want to sell them starting immediately after Thanksgiving and all through December.

When trying to decide what to sell during the holidays, research food trends to see what's "in" this year. This can easily be done by doing some online research, reading cooking/baking magazines and visiting other bakeries in your area.

Taking Special Orders for Holidays

You need to think about when people will want to have items for specific holidays and plan ahead. For example, for Thanksgiving orders, you're probably going to have a lot of people wanting items for the big day, so you should plan to take orders beginning mid November for pickup the Wednesday before. The same goes for Christmas and probably Easter. For holidays such as Halloween, you'll probably get orders all month long at a steady pace. This is something you'll most likely have to learn as you go, but you should try to plan as much as possible for the best results.

Order Policy

So you've decided what to sell, now it's time to figure out how your customers will place orders. You have several options when it comes to this:

- ◆ Phone orders

- ◆ Online orders

- ◆ Email orders

- ◆ In person, such as at farmer's markets

You can do one of these or all of these. My recommendation is to make it as easy as possible for a customer to place an order. You'll also need to let them know how soon they'll get a response. For example, if they email an order to you on Monday, they need to know that they'll get a response within 24 hours, and then according to your production schedule, their item will be available on Wednesday. You can let them know that by calling you during your business hours, they'll get the fastest response; you'll just have to make sure you always answer your phone during those hours.

For in-person orders, you should have an order form that they can easily fill out and give back to you. If you have pickup at your house, you should strongly discourage customers to show up at your door to place orders, although this is up to you. Whatever you decide to do, you have to let your customers know, and be consistent. If you state that you respond to all emails or phone calls within 24 hours, then you should follow through with that *every time*. Don't want to return calls or emails on Sundays? Make that your policy.

Regarding online orders: If you are going to take orders online via your website, you need to have a policy dictating when those orders will be ready. It's also a good idea to let your customer know you will contact them within a certain amount of time after the order is placed (say 24 hours) to verify the order. This way, if something goes wrong (the site locked up, the information didn't get transmitted, whatever it is), they'll know to contact you if they haven't received notification of the order. Again, it's a good idea to let customers know that phone calls will garner the fastest response.

Rush Orders

Whether you want to do rush orders is up to you; many people do these and add a surcharge on them. Rush orders are great for customer convenience and from a financial standpoint, but this means you have to have a way to fit them in your production schedule. My advice is that if you are going to do rush orders, have a clear-cut policy about them, and that then you set aside time in your schedule in case you get them. If you can't fill them, you will only make your customers mad.

Just make sure you clearly state your rush order policy. They'll need to make a phone call; and orders placed before xx time will be available at xx. If you want to guarantee you'll have a day off a week, you should state that you don't do rush orders on Sunday (or whatever day).

Minimum Orders

If someone wants one cookie, can you accommodate that? If you are at the farmer's market, you probably can, but if they simply want one or two items for a special order, this can be a pain since you are not a retail bakery. The best way to handle this is to state an order minimum for special orders, and package items how you want to sell them at markets and craft shows. While you may think a dollar amount is good for special order minimums, think about what you are going to do if someone wants one of this and one of that.

Pickup and Delivery Schedule

After you've decided on when you're going to bake what items, next it's time to figure out how your customers will get them. You have several options, including having them pick them up at your house or other location, or you can deliver if that's something you want to take on. Whatever you do, you want it to be easy to understand, as well as consistent. One of the biggest mistakes new business owners make is trying to please customers by straying from their policies. This will only cause you stress.

Before you make your first sale, you need to create your pickup and delivery schedule and then stick to it. Keep in mind when your customers are likely to want your items; if you sell birthday cakes, you'd be committing a major error not to have your items available for weekends. You want to make the majority of your customers happy, while also creating a schedule that works for you.

Payment

Your customer has placed their order and scheduled their pickup. Now how are they going to pay for their products? You should have a very clear payment policy that your customers understand before they place their order. You should accept cash and credit cards, of course, but what about checks? Accepting checks is entirely up to you, but you should think about the demographic of your customer. While most young people probably don't write checks, a lot of older people still do and may not have debit cards. While you don't want to turn customers away, there is a greater risk to taking checks. Whether you want to take that risk is up to you.

For website orders, you can accept PayPal as well. Many people like this option because they don't have to give you their banking information; PayPal acts as an intermediary. It's easy to set up, and is very cost effective.

You also need to think about whether you want to require partial or full payment up front, especially for large orders. In the beginning, you will likely rely only on special orders; if someone doesn't show up, you may not be able to recoup the time and money you've got into the products. If you're unsure, you can start by requiring a deposit up front for large orders. Most people will not mind this, especially since you are a new business, and you're not mass-producing items for sale later.

Refund Policy

You will need to have some kind of guarantee for your products. While you probably aren't really going to take your baked goods back, what if someone is unhappy with something? You need to be clear about your refund policy. You can state that you'll replace or refund anything your customer is unhappy with; you can even state no refunds (although I don't recommend it). Most customers will be happy just knowing that you stand by your product, and will gladly accept a replacement. I would make it a goal to make sure that your customers are always happy. Is the cost of replacement product or a refund worth the loss of a customer? Probably not.

Freshness and Storage

How are you going to store your products? How long will they stay fresh? You customer will ask these questions, and you should have an answer. They'll also want to know when your items were baked, and you should be honest. If you can bake and sell the same day, you should, but you should never sell something more than one day after you've baked it.

How Much Should You Bake?

This is one of the biggest challenges of all bakers, and one that you will struggle with throughout your career as a baker. You don't want to make too much for fear of throwing it away, but too little and you're losing sales. In terms of customer satisfaction, baking too much is your best bet.

In a perfect world, all of your customers will order what they want, so you can just make it, sell it and not have leftovers. Unfortunately, it's not a perfect world, and it will likely not work this way. As you get going, it will get easier, but you will likely never be able to consistently make the right amount.

Some tips:

◆ If you're going to sell at farmer's markets, craft bazaars or local stores, visit the locations beforehand and see what kind of business they get. You can even ask other vendors about their sales.

◆ Try to work with local stores that will buy your products for a flat rate; that way you don't have to worry about whether they sell.

◆ Think about your expenses, and how much you have to sell to break even. This is a good place to start, and a good goal to have in the beginning.

◆ Encourage customers to place orders, but don't expect everyone to comply. You can let them know the benefits of placing orders (they get what they want at the time they want it, you won't run out of what they want), but remember that in a day and age where people are used to being able to pick up whatever they want at the supermarket, it can be hard to train them otherwise.

Once you start baking and selling, you'll have a much better idea of how much to make, although it may always be somewhat of a trial and error process.

Customer Feedback

This is the most important aspect of your business and one that you should always take seriously. In the beginning, you may be surprised to find that your favorite item to make is actually your lowest seller, and those cookies that you think are just so-so are the ones that your customers love.

You always want to keep up with your customer feedback, otherwise, you won't know what your customers like and want to purchase. It doesn't matter how much you like something, if your customer doesn't, you won't make any money.

How can you get customer feedback? Ask them. You'll probably get a good idea what they want when you see which product is selling the most, but there is no better way to hear what you customers want than to hear it straight from them.

- Create a customer satisfaction survey, and offer a free item (such as a cookie) to those who fill it out. Many people will be happy to help, and getting valuable customer feedback will be worth the cost of the item you are giving away. Ask questions such as what is their favorite item on the menu, what they would like to see, and questions relating to overall quality and value. Encourage honesty even if it is negative; it's the only way to get a clear picture of your customer appeal.

- Make giving feedback easy. Don't provide them with a two-page survey that they have to fill out immediately upon receiving it; instead make it short and to the point, and let them know that they can return it to you at their convenience. If you hand them a survey at the farmer's market or other location, have some pens handy so they can fill it out with ease.

- If you ask for feedback, listen to it. Don't ask because you want them to think that you care, actually listen and take action if you can. If a lot of people ask for a certain product, try creating it. Let all customers know that the product in question was created because of customers like them who made suggestions.

This shows that you will use customer feedback, and encourages customers to give you an opinion.

- If you get negative feedback, respond immediately. Handle complaints fairly and professionally. Don't give in to unreasonable demands; instead talk in a calm voice, ask the customer what they would like you to do, and make a fair offer. Remember, you can't and won't please everyone. You can only do what you can do.

- When testing a new product, make some samples, and offer them to customers before you sell them. Ask what they think, and record these answers.

- Always let your customers know that you encourage feedback, but don't be too pushy.

- Be your own customer. Take some time and walk through the entire process of ordering, pickup/delivery, using your website, etc. Going through the whole process yourself will allow you to see the process through your customers' eyes, and make changes as necessary if something isn't convenient, or if there's an unnecessary step in the process that can be removed.

Now that you've got your policies and procedures implemented, it's time to make a sale!

Chapter 4

Sales

Now that you have a product that you love and that knocks everyone's socks off, the next step is getting that product out to the masses, and making some sales!

Many home bakers begin their business selling to family and friends, which is a great tactic since they are your biggest fans. The problem is that doing that takes a while to get started, and no matter how many people you know personally, you probably don't know enough to sustain a business long term, so you're going to have to branch out and find customers elsewhere.

How are you going to do that? Well there are many ways to do that and we're going to go over them all. You don't want to limit yourself when trying to sell your products, and you want to get them out there in any way you can.

In this chapter we're going to go over the various methods of selling including:

- ◆ Farmer's markets
- ◆ Craft bazaars and community events
- ◆ Online via your website
- ◆ Online via third party sites
- ◆ Local supermarkets and grocery stores

Pricing

Before we do that though, you're going to take a quick course in pricing your products. Pricing is perhaps one of the hardest parts of selling any good, and can set the stage for who will buy your products and what their value is now and in the future. The price determines they type of person who will buy your goods and it doesn't always have to do with money. Confused? Let me explain.

People buy all kinds of things for many reasons and you are never going to understand them all. Think about products you buy every day. You're probably looking for a few things, such as high-quality products that fill your needs at a price that is reasonable. No matter what the product, there is always a range of prices, from expensive to cheap, and they attract different types of customers. This is where you have to ask yourself what you are selling and what kind of customer you are trying to attract. Before determining the exact price for your items, you have to first decide where you will be on the scale as far as range, and this is something only you can decide. Let's take a look at the differences.

High Prices

While this may not be the most effective pricing strategy it does work for many reasons. There are many people who have money and who believe that price alone determines the quality and value of the products they buy, and baked goods are certainly no exception. While of course price alone does not set value, it can work to your advantage. There are pros and cons to this type of pricing, but in order for it to work, you have to give your customer something extra special, and market to a different crowd.

For starters, you'll have greater profits, which means you don't have to sell as many products to make as much money. This is a great advantage, except that you will not sell nearly as many products. Some people simply will not pay astronomical prices for your products no matter how good they are and what you offer them, so you'll have to work extra hard to find those that will. You'll also have to constantly defend your prices to a good variety of customers that will pay them, but only if they feel they are getting something special. Unfortunately, the group of people who will buy any product simply because of high prices is small, and probably not enough to sustain a business long term.

Average

This is where you'll find run-of-the-mill products. It's the easiest pricing structure but can get you lost in a sea of other baked goods. Price is the way many products stand out, and if your prices are the same as everyone else in your area, you'll have to do something else to make your products shine.

Low Prices

Super low prices can be the death of a small business, and can be a grave mistake many make in the beginning hoping to get customers in the door. The idea is that they can then raise the prices on them once they've got a large customer base. This is a terrible strategy and one you should avoid. Why?

- If you sell items at low prices, you'll make low profits. This means that you'll sell a lot, which is good, but you'll be working overtime to fill a lot of orders for not a lot of money.

- You will be known as a bargain bakery, which can make it hard to raise prices, even a little bit, without losing the majority of your customer base. If you change the one thing that makes you stand out, suddenly people won't have a reason to go back.

- Low profit margin means errors can be costly.

Okay, so how the heck are you supposed to price your products knowing all this information? Well, you should start by first figuring out exactly what it costs to make each product. Get out your trusty notebook, receipts for ingredients and a calculator, and figure out the cost of the ingredients for each individual product. Once you've done this, you'll probably come up with a pretty low amount per item, but you have to realize that you've only got the ingredients in so far. You've also got to include:

- Your time/labor

- Overhead costs (packaging, labels, etc.)

- Utilities (you'll be running your oven way more than you ever have)

- Personal needs (health and liability insurance, etc.)

How do you calculate all of those things? You're probably not going to be able to calculate them down to a tee, but you have to think about what you are providing your customers, and who your ideal customer is. What is the median income for your targeted customer base? If you live in a middle class area, you'll probably have a hard time getting your customers to pay high prices, but if you're in an affluent area it may be hard to sell low-priced products. It all depends on what the market will bear. You also have to keep in mind that you aren't making mass-produced products; you're selling homemade goods in a local setting. This may make your products worth more to some customers. It helps to note that some things are worth much more. Cake decorating, for example is a skill that most people don't have. It takes years to master, and people will pay high prices for exceptional work. Chocolate chip cookies, on the other hand, are something many people can and will bake themselves before paying someone else a high price to do it for them, even if the cookies are the best they've ever had.

An exercise that may prove helpful is to visit local bakeries in the area and take notes on the highest and lowest priced items. What do these bakeries offer? What makes certain items special besides price?

Unfortunately there is no magic formula that makes pricing easier. The bottom line is that you have to set a price that covers all of your costs, is right for the area in which you are selling, and is satisfying to your customers. Remember, you can't please everyone, and no matter where you are on the pricing scale, you will be too high or too low for someone. Just remember to set your price and stick to it. Don't let customers who tell you they can get a comparable product cheaper elsewhere (unless they *all* say this; then you may need to rethink your strategy) scare you into lowering your prices. Use common sense, create a high-quality product for great value and don't look back.

One final tip regarding pricing: Don't try to be both an upscale and a bargain bakery thinking you can please the masses; it just doesn't work. Customers looking for luxury want to buy items that other people can't afford, while all it takes for those looking for a deal is one overpriced item to make them run for the hills. This goes all the way back to the beginning where I told you to choose your niche and stick to it. It's better to be known for one thing than try to do it all.

Got your prices set? Let's start making some sales!

Selling in Person

Selling in person is an easy way to meet your customers, talk about your business and create a presence in your community. There are several ways to do this.

Farmer's Markets

Farmer's markets are perhaps one of the best ways to sell homemade baked goods, and with the increasing popularity in buying local products, farmer's markets are practically everywhere. Most communities host markets every week during the warmer months, and many even have them in the winter as well. Before you just jump in, there are some things you should know about farmer's markets:

- If you're new to farmers' markets, they began as a way for local farmers to gather and sell all of their local produce. Now many markets will accept booths from any merchant that makes handmade products, and while most are food and edibles, you can often find jewelry and craft items as well.

- Most markets have strict rules regarding their application process and what you can sell. They'll also have a cut off date for last applications. For bigger markets, this can be months in advance, so you'll want to start planning several months ahead, especially if it's your first year. You'll need to be thinking about what you want to sell in the winter to get ready for the summer.

- The cost of selling is probably higher than you may expect. You'll have to have tables and probably a tent in case of rain, as well as a way to transport all of your products to the market. You'll have to pay a fee for each market you attend. The rules are different for every one. Some will allow you to participate in as many or few sessions as you'd like, while some will require a whole season. You can expect to pay anywhere from $25 or more per session, with busy markets costing more than double that. Also, some markets will require you to have liability insurance as well, which can be several hundred dollars per year, even if you're only using it for a few months. On the plus side, if you do more than one market, the insurance should cover them all. Check with your agent for details.

- Many people who visit farmer's markets are health conscious and have a picture of what types of products they'll buy. Baked goods do sell really well, but generally patrons are looking for "rustic" or "artisan" items like breads, pies and quick breads. Fancy decorated cookies, cakes and high-end pastries that are high in fat and calories may not sell quite as well as you think.

- Many people go to farmer's markets looking for bargains, and while you will find people who will pay a fair price for quality products made with good ingredients, you may not be able to sell a lot of "luxury" type items.

Before deciding to sell at local markets, it's a good idea to visit the various markets in your area. See what they're selling, and how many people are there. It may be a good idea to visit markets where someone isn't already selling what you offer to avoid competition. You should then contact those that are in charge of the various markets in your community to determine pricing and which ones are going to be best for you. To start out, it may not be a great idea to sign on for a whole season; if you can do one or two events to get your feet wet, this may be a better option.

Craft Bazaars and Other Community Events 50

Craft shows and bazaars, bake sales and other commun
places to sell products, get your name out and attract new cus......
are very similar to farmer's markets except that instead of a weekly event, they
are often single events spread out throughout the year, such as during the
holidays. You'll need to plan way in advance, and of course pay registration
fees, and have the proper set up. It can be difficult to gauge how successful
you'll be since different events have different turnouts, and it can be hard to
visit them to plan for something a year in advance. The best way to find them
is to talk to people in your area, visit as many events as you can, and see how
your business will fit in. Remember the costs involved as well; you'll have
registration fees, required set up and insurance, as necessary.

General Tips For Selling At Farmer's Markets, Craft Bazaars and Community Events:

- Selling in person is a great way to meet your customers and get feedback. Be ready to answer questions about your business, your product and anything else that may come up. Be positive about everything and be as friendly as possible. You are the face of your business; if you're not enthusiastic about your products, how can you expect your customers to be?

- Make extra products so that you can provide samples. In many cases, this can make the difference between making a sale and not, and the amount you'll spend doing this is minimal compared to what you'll gain.

- As far as payment methods, most people know to bring cash to these events, but it's easy to take credit cards these days if you have a smart phone or even PayPal account. Check into companies like Square of Jumio, which will allow you to accept credit cards with your phone. It's not absolutely necessary, but it can mean the difference between a customer buying from you or a competitor.

- Make sure you have plenty of business cards and copies of your menu if you don't have everything you offer available. This way your customers can place special orders, especially for farmer's markets where they can pick up at next week's event. It takes some of the pressure off guessing how much you'll have to make.

Selling Online

Selling your products online is a whole different ball game with a different set of rules. There are many ways to do it, whether you are simply taking orders for pick up, or shipping them across the country. It can be a bit overwhelming at first, especially if you're not especially tech friendly. It doesn't have to be difficult though, which is good, because in this day and age, an online presence is a necessity.

Your Own Site

Online sales aside, you need to have your own website. It doesn't have to be fancy, but it does have to include basic information about you and your business: your menu, contact information, your policies, and how your customers can buy your products. The first thing many people will do when they hear about local baker selling products in their neighborhood is search for them online, and if you're not there, they may quickly lose interest. We'll go over more about getting set up in the next chapter, but it's something you have to do.

Creating a website is not very difficult, and if you're even a little bit tech savvy you can probably do it yourself unless you need something special. If you don't want to try on your own, you can find local or even online designers who can do it for as little as a few hundred dollars.

Once you have your domain name, you'll need to decide if you are going to sell your products on your site. You have several options to do this. You can have your customers complete the sale online, where they'll select the product, pay for it and have it shipped, or you can have them place the order then pay in-person upon pickup. These options all require different types of web design, so you'll need to talk to your designer about your options.

If you decide to sell your items online to be shipped nationally, you'll need to do heavy marketing in order for people to find your site. This may require knowledge and expertise that you don't quite have.

Third Party Sites

There are several third party websites where you can sell your products through these sites and ship them. Etsy is a site that allows users to list and sell homemade products of any kind, not just food, while Foodzie is one that caters to those selling food and edible items. There are pros and cons to using these sites.

Pros:

- These sites are very similar to eBay where you can easily list your item in their database and users find them and purchase by searching for them. While you will still need to do some marketing, these sites do their own advertising and mass marketing so you'll have somewhat of a built-in customer base.

- You can get started and set up in no time and have your items up and running almost as fast as you can type them in. You can list as many items as you want.

- Unless you are selling a really high volume of products, you'll only pay when you sell, and the fees are usually fair for these types of sites.

- On sites like Etsy, you can pay to have your item featured on the homepage, leading to more sales than ever.

Cons:

- There's a lot of competition. If you search on Etsy for "cupcakes," a lot of listings will come up, and your listing may be buried in a sea of others.

- Shipping food items can be expensive, and for that reason, many people simply won't do it.

- Just because you list your items on these highly recognized sites does not mean you will automatically have a lot of sales. You still have to promote yourself.

- Selling in person and online for shipment is almost like a different business. Yes, the products are the same, but the marketing and packaging are very different. Plan to invest a lot of time in it to be successful.

General Tips For Selling Online:

- No matter where you're going to sell your products, you'll need to take photographs. It can be extremely difficult to take appealing picture of food, even beautiful baked goods, so you should experiment until you master it, or consider taking a digital photography class. A clear, well-lit photo can make a sale on its own, and you should not forget that. Even if you don't plan to sell online, you should put some nice photos on your own site. If you can't do it yourself, consider hiring a professional. It makes a difference.

- Learn to write mouthwatering descriptions. Even though your photographs may be beautiful, you still need to describe your products in a way that makes someone think they have to have it. A well-written description plus a lovely photograph will translate to a sale, and once they've tasted your product, they'll be back for more.

- Shipping will always be a challenge when selling food items online because you want your items to arrive fresh, but this means you'll have to require rush shipping. You should set your shipping policies up front. Personally, if I were going to ship online, I would require overnight or two-day delivery (depending on the item). If you allow your customer to save money on shipping and the item arrives less than fresh, they'll blame you even though it's not your fault, which can harm your reputation. Whatever you decide, state your policy and stick to it.

◆ State your policies regarding when you bake and when you ship, so your customers know exactly when to expect their item and how fresh it will be. You should always bake the item as close to shipment as possible to allow for delays in delivery (it happens), and ensure freshness. Send your customer an email once it has shipped letting them know when to expect it.

◆ State your policies regarding returns or what you will do in the event an item arrives less fresh than you had hoped. If there is a delay in the delivery service (such as the post office delivering later than expected), you should replace the item, even if it is not your fault. This is why shipping overnight is always best; it's guaranteed, and the customer must sign for it. This is really the best way to go to avoid problems; it is expensive, and will turn off a lot of customers, but it's the best way to avoid problems and a bad reputation. Also think about shipping refunds. If you are replacing an item, you'll probably pay shipping for that, but if you're giving a refund, are you going to refund the shipping costs the customer has already paid? Hopefully this won't come up often, but you should have a policy set if it does.

◆ Make sure your items are packed properly. They should be completely cool before being wrapped and packed, and packaged in a way that ensures they will arrive just as beautifully as if they were purchased in person.

◆ Consider adding a handwritten note with your package, and always include a copy of your menu and a business card with every order.

- If you're selling on a third party site such as Etsy, encourage the customer to leave positive feedback.

A last thought on selling online: While we live in a digital age, and practically anything can be sold online, you need to ask yourself why your customers would buy your products online as opposed to buying from a local bakery or grocery store, especially when you factor in shipping costs and wait times for delivery. You'll need to offer something extra special that your customers can't get elsewhere in order for them to justify the hassle. If you can't do that, then maybe you should focus on selling your products locally for the time being.

Selling Products Wholesale at Local Grocery Stores, Supermarkets and Restaurants

People love buying locally made products, and many businesses are taking note by trying to partner with local businesses to offer their customers a variety of options. It's easier than you think.

While you'll have to lower your prices, there are benefits to wholesale:

- You'll be getting your name out there. Many customers who visit these businesses will see or hear about your business and products.

- You'll have standing orders that you can count on.

- You'll make excellent contacts in your community.

- If your products are a success, it's a great way to get your foot in the door to national retailers.

Grocery Stores and Supermarkets

While you probably will have a tough time getting your products in the biggest supermarket chains in your area (although you never know unless you ask!), you may be able to get your products into a smaller local store or a store that specializes in local products.

Start by visiting local stores in your area and seeing what types of products they sell. See if there is a particular type of product that seems to do well and if your products fit the bill.

Talk to whomever is in charge of putting products in the store. You may have a lot of competition from other local merchants competing for shelf space, so make sure you are prepared to explain why you are a good fit. Show them your menu and wlebsite, and be ready to divulge your sales numbers if necessary.

Ask how payment arrangements and pricing decisions are made. Depending on the size of the store, they may want to pay you after your items have sold; this can be risky on your part. Ideally you want to provide them with the products that they pay you for and then sell, but you want to know up front how much they are going to sell your products for. If they are going to sell them for a price that is too high, it can turn off any future customers from buying from you individually because they think you are too expensive.

Try not to put your products in stores that don't move a lot of products. Doing so can result in customers buying baked goods that aren't necessarily at the peak of freshness. This can result in an unhappy customer – even if it's not your fault. Be clear about how long your baked goods will last before agreeing to anything, even if the store is paying you upfront.

Make sure your products are clearly labeled with the name of your business and your contact information. If the merchant won't allow this, then you should consider selling your products elsewhere. After all, this is one of the biggest benefits of selling in stores.

Restaurants and Coffee Shops

Local restaurants are a great way to sell your products and reach customers in a different type of setting. Many restaurant owners love this option because it's something they don't have to worry about, whether it's bread or desserts.

The process for finding restaurants to sell in is similar to finding grocery stores. You want to start with smaller places and simply ask where they get their products. If they don't prepare them in house, inform them of the benefits of having a local person do it, as opposed to buying frozen/prepared products.

Small coffee shops are perfect for selling pastries and breakfast items, and many would love to work with local bakers as opposed to buying products that are already prepared.

Tips For Selling Wholesale:

♦ When pricing for wholesale, remember that although the merchant selling your products has to make a profit, so do you. Price your items fairly and ask what the merchant will be selling your product for.

♦ The most important thing is that no matter where you are selling, you are getting credit for your products. This can be in the form of packaging, a waiter mentioning you, your name on a menu, or business cards being handed out to customers. Always ask up front how your items will be presented, and make sure you are kept in the loop regarding any changes to the process.

♦ Make sure that the merchant selling your products knows the shelf life of your items and that they must not sell or distribute beyond that timeframe.

♦ Make sure you understand payment arrangements and delivery schedules ahead of time. You don't want to get stuck for items that aren't sold/used.

◆ Set minimum orders. Since you are selling wholesale items for less, you want to know it will be worthwhile to you.

◆ While the idea of selling to businesses all over town is appealing, don't take on so many wholesale accounts that you don't have time for your individual customers.

Now that you've got the hang of selling your products, the next step is marketing. In the next chapter, you'll learn how to create a brand for your business and where to get all those customers.

Chapter 5

Branding

Branding is basically creating your identity as a business. It's about crafting the image or message that you are trying to convey to your customers. In this chapter, we're going to walk you through the process, including:

- Deciding what your public image will be in the business

- Creating a logo and promotional materials that clearly define your business

- Creating a website

- Packaging your products in a way that makes you stand out

Branding is essentially what sets you apart from your competitors, and it's what makes people associate your company and products with good things. Unfortunately, this doesn't happen on its own.

If you've never been in business for yourself, you may not be aware of how much these things mean to your bottom line, but hopefully by the end of this chapter you'll see that your brand is what will make customers choose you over your competitors, and it will become what defines your business, even more than your products in some cases. So if you're ready to get started, let's get going!

Your Image

How do you want your customers to see you? Do you want to be the face of your business? Do you want to get to know your customers personally? This is all part of branding and creating an image and there are many ways to go. You don't have to be the face of your business, you can simply sell your products to your customers without a lot of interaction, or you can plaster your photo on everything and become a public spokesperson for your brand. This is entirely up to you, and you can be successful either way.

What do you want your customers to think of when they think of you and your business? A grandma standing at the stove baking, or a young housewife who bakes while surrounded by her children and manages to pull it off? You should tie it all in to your products as well. You have to keep all of these things in mind when creating your brand and your image.

Keep in mind that as the owner of a business, you are going to have to take on a somewhat public role. If there is a review in the newspaper or other local publication, you may be quoted for example. No matter what your image is, you want to stand by your products and your business and never act ashamed.

Logo

A logo is a simple image that your customers will associate with your business. Your logo will be on pretty much everything that you put out there, so it should be something that clearly states what you're all about. This can be difficult to achieve, but it's really important. It should be on your business cards, letterhead, website, menus and anything else that you have created to represent your business. Although it may take awhile, you want your customers to associate your logo with your business and your products.

There are several ways to go when deciding what your logo will look like, and although many logos have the name of the business in them, you don't necessarily have to include it. If you have some graphic design experience, you can try creating it yourself, but if not, a professional is best.

If you're new to this kind of thing, you'll find that when seeking professional design services, you have options ranging in price depending on whom you hire and what you're asking them to do. You can get a logo designed for as little as a hundred dollars or a complete branding package for thousands. What you choose will depend on a lot of factors, including your budget, but you must consider the following when making your decision:

♦ Your logo will be the first thing many people see when they learn of your business. A poorly designed or boring logo probably won't translate to a bad experience, but will the same customer remember you next time? Probably not.

♦ You want your logo to work on a wide variety of things, including printed material, such as business cards, as well as on the Web and even on T-shirts if necessary.

♦ Your logo must convey the same message whether on a tiny business card or a large banner.

♦ Your logo should look good in color and in black and white.

With these things in mind, you want something that is original and creative, yet also simple. The lowest priced designer may simply take a clip art image and attach it to a generic font that will not say what you want it to. An expensive designer will sit down with you and ask you about your business, your product and the image you are trying to project. He'll give you several options and styles, and the process may take awhile. Is it worth the money? Maybe not in the beginning, especially if you're on a tight budget, but you should definitely consider something in the middle if you can afford it. You can always "re-brand" in the future, but it's much easier to establish a brand than it is to change an existing one.

Whether you decide to hire someone or do it yourself, you should keep these things in mind when coming up with a logo:

♦ It should not use more than three colors

♦ It should be recognizable

- It should be original; do not try to use another company's logo or a "piece" of it

- Try to avoid clip art or anything else that someone else may use

- An image is OK; a photo is not

While these aren't the only rules, these are things to consider when deciding on a logo. Once you've got it narrowed down, ask other people what they think. What is the first thing they see? What words do they think of?

While your logo isn't the only thing that will sell your business, you should not overlook the importance of it.

Website

If you are not too web savvy, you may be thinking you don't really need a website, but I'm going to be blunt: You are wrong. Even the most technophobic use the Web on a daily basis, and whether you want to believe it or not, the Internet is here to stay. If you are going to be in business, you must have a website. This is especially true if you don't plan on having a retail outlet in which your customers can walk in and ask questions. How will they find you? How will they know what you sell? How will they place orders?

Like logo design, there are many avenues to take when deciding on a website, but before you know what your next step will be, you must decide what you want your website to do. Your website can be as simple as a one-page explanation of who you are and how to get in touch, or a full-service site where visitors can come and place orders for delivery or pickup. You can even add a blog where you can update customers on new products and news about your business. You have a wide range of options, and the good news is, creating and managing a website isn't nearly as costly or as difficult as you may think. To determine what your site will look like, ask yourself the following questions:

- Do you want your customers to be able to place orders online? You can have a set up where a customer places an order and it is emailed directly to you after they place it. You can even use a credit card merchant or PayPal to have them pay you in advance. PayPal is easy to set up by going to the website and registering; you can be taking credit card payments in a few minutes.

◆ Do you want to place orders to be shipped? If your customers are going to simply place orders for local pickup, you can have them pay when they pick up their goods; if you're going to ship items, you must get payment beforehand by credit card or PayPal.

◆ How much time do you want to spend on the website? If you aren't particularly Internet savvy, a simple informational site will do; if you don't mind getting your hands dirty, you should consider blogging, using social media sites like Facebook, and other methods of updating your site on a regular basis. A website can be the best advertising you have for your business, so you should take advantage of it if you can. You can interact with many people online, through forums and feeds, and get to know a lot of your customers personally this way.

A good website:

◆ Is easy to use. You want your customers to be able to find what they are looking for easily. What will most people be looking for when they come to your site? Probably your menu and contact information. You want these to be easy to find.

◆ Is easy to read. While you may like the idea of yellow font on a green background, will someone be able to read it without getting a headache? Keep it simple. Use colors and fonts that are easy to read.

◆ Has mouthwatering photos and descriptions that will help products sell themselves.

◆ Shows off your personality and the image you are trying to create without being hard to use or hard to read.

- Doesn't have a lot of annoying features such as flash animations and automatic music. Remember, many people will have the goal of getting the information they are looking for as quickly as possible; you don't want to slow them down with useless content.

At the bare minimum your website should include:

- An "About" section telling who you are and how you decided to go into business

- Your full menu, including photographs and descriptions

- Contact information, including how to place and pick up orders

- Your policies regarding processing times and returns

- A way for customers to sign up for your email list

- A FAQ section with questions and answers about your products and policies. Many people will come here first to read all of the information in one place.

If you want to establish more of a presence on the Web, you could include:

- The ability for customers to place orders for pickup

- The ability to accept payment for those orders through credit cards or PayPal

For advanced Web users who want to get the most out of their website, you can:

- Sell your baked goods online nationwide for delivery

- Post daily or weekly blog posts letting your customers know all about what's going on with the bakery

- Add connections to your Facebook and Twitter pages

You need to consider that updating and maintaining a website with blogging and nationwide orders is a lot of work, but it can translate into sales.

The Look of Your Website

Once you've decided what you want your website to do, you have to decide how you want it to look. You should have your logo by now, so you can add that. But there are a lot of other things to consider, such as placement of various menu bars, and page options. Consider color as well. A good web designer will walk you through all of these options.

Choosing a Domain Name

Your domain name is the address of your site, and the address that visitors will use to find your website. Choosing a domain name is easy if your first choice is available, but very often it is not. The best choice is the name of your bakery, such as www.yourbakery.com, but if that isn't available (and it may not be), you'll need to choose something else. Don't choose wildly though. Use the following tips for choosing a good domain name:

- Know the basics about domains. For example, .com is the most common general domain, and should be your first choice. Others include .org (usually used for organizations and charities), and .gov (government websites). There is also .info, which is good for information and .me is often used for personal blogs. You should avoid these, as most people won't remember them. If you can't find a .com name, then .net will suffice, but only as a last resort.

- Your domain name should be short and easy to remember, but it should also be unique. You don't want your site to be easily confused with another site; you do want it to be easy for visitors to enter into the URL bar. For example: www.barbarasbakery.com is easy to remember, while www.barbarassmalltownbakeryandbreadshop.com is probably too much.

- Avoid using strings of random numbers and symbols such as dashes if you can help it.

- Try to make the name something that will instantly give your visitors an idea of what you do.

- Don't choose a name with misspelled words such as "kupcake."

- Don't use a name that is copyrighted by someone else. Check with www.copyright.gov before purchasing a domain name just to be sure.

- You may find that the exact domain name you want is available but very expensive. People often buy up names and hold on to them until someone is willing to pay a crazy high price. Only you can decide if it's worth it to you to pay a huge sum for the right name.

Choosing a domain name is similar to choosing a name for your business: It should be memorable, describe your personality and image, and easy for customers to find.

Website Design

Like logo design, web design comes in many forms. With the popularity of the Internet these days, many people do web design as side work, and a lot of people use software and programs to design a site themselves. While this may be the least expensive option, it's not always the best. Where do you get started?

- First, do some searches for similar businesses. They don't have to be in your area; they can be anywhere since you aren't buying anything. Take a look at some sites and see what you like and what you don't like. Ask family and friends to do the same. Get a general consensus of what will work best for you.

- If you know someone who does web design, ask him or her for advice and a price quote. Be careful about having a friend do the work for you, unless you are willing to strongly state what you want and what changes need to be made even if it may cause hurt feelings.

◆ If you paid someone to do your logo and you are satisfied with their work, ask them if they do websites. A lot of designers will do packages and you can save money by having more than one service.

◆ Don't forget about hosting. You'll have to pay someone to host your site, probably a monthly fee. It's not very much, and most designers can help you with hosting. If you're selling your products online, you'll probably have additional fees, including those that come with credit card processing.

Like logo design, the costs for web design can vary greatly depending on what features you need, and what you want it to look like. While you probably don't need the best and most expensive designers out there, you have to remember that since you don't have a storefront where your customers can walk into to get a feel for your business, your website is the first interaction they may have with you. Just as you wouldn't want a physical location to be dirty, ugly or laid out poorly, you don't want your website to be either. Sometimes the only way to achieve this is by hiring a professional. It's worth the money.

Can You Do It Yourself?

The short answer is yes, you can create your own website, and many software programs make it easy to do. Should you? That's up to you. If you have basic design experience, a good eye and can get it done relatively quickly, then it may be cost effective to try to do it on your own. If you have a hard time surfing the web, and don't know exactly what features attract customers, chances are trying to do it yourself will be frustrating, time consuming, and something best left to someone else. Time spent doing this is time you are taking away from more important things.

Attracting Visitors

The final thing you have to keep in mind when creating a website – whether you do it or someone else does it – is that getting your site up is only half the battle. Once it's up, how are people going to find you? Many people who are not Web savvy believe that setting up your website will attract business. Unfortunately, nothing could be further from the truth.

While someone searching for your specific site will have no problem finding you as long as they know your domain name or the name of your bakery, what about someone who is simply looking for bakeries in your city or cupcakes in your city? Doing a search for these items will turn up hundreds or thousands of search results. Chances are you won't be on the first page, and if that's the case, the person looking will most likely never find you.

How do you get your name at the top of the search results? This is a complicated answer, but it basically involves using key search terms to rig the search engines to put you on top. There are a lot of factors, it's a fairly complicated process, and one that will involve research, time and techniques you may not understand.

So what do you do? Well, this is where a professional design company can often help you. Web designers know that once the design is done and the website is up you'll still need to get traffic, so they offer Search Engine Optimization (SEO) packages that will get you the traffic you need. This basically means they'll do all the research (such as finding out just what your customers are searching for), and help to implement those terms into your website.

For these reasons, hiring a professional is probably a good idea, unless you want to add another item to your busy schedule. Of course you can find someone to do your SEO for you even if they didn't design your site, but remember that many companies will have packages and give you discounts for a variety of services. So if you have someone do your logo, website design and maintenance, and SEO, you'll get a break.

The bottom line about having a website is that it's only effective if people see it. If they do, it can be an amazing marketing tool, especially since you're not going to have a lot of options without having an actual storefront. Most people these days use the Web to find information, so you want to be there when they search.

There are other ways of attracting visitors to your site, some of which you can do yourself:

- Put your website address on every piece of printed material you create: business cards, paper menus, flyers, print ads, packaging, etc.

- Visit bakery forums and blogs relating to your topic. Make relevant comments and include your website address. It's best to create a persona at these places and add information that is necessary; otherwise, you'll simply look like spam. This is not at all what you want, and can backfire.

- Attach a blog to your site. This increases traffic and allows you to get to know your customers. Having a blog also means you'll have more content, which means your site will be much more easily picked up by search engines. A one-page information site makes it difficult to use lots of keywords without taking away from the overall quality of your site. More content equals much more opportunity for keyword placement.

One final tip about your website: Proofread it, proofread it again, and have several close family members and friends proofread it before you go live. One tiny mistake can seem unprofessional to some people and take away from all of your hard work. If you can't write content that flows, consider hiring someone who can.

Packaging

We've already touched on packaging in previous chapters, but now we're going to talk about how presenting and packaging and your products can make a huge difference in your overall brand.

Packaging is one of those things that doesn't necessarily contribute to the quality of the product, but definitely makes or breaks an item's success.

Have you ever had to make a decision between two products (such as wine or gourmet cookies) and chosen one over the other solely because of packaging? Many people do exactly this, and you should take advantage of it.

Before we start, let's take a look at what goes into packaging:

- Boxes and bags, both plastic and paper

- Labels

- Ribbons, twist ties or stickers to keep packages sealed

- Bakery tissues to prevent food from touching both your hands and the package

As a general rule, your packaging should be:

- Attractive

- Inexpensive

- Memorable

- A good representation of your business and your products

Is this easy to achieve? Maybe. The hardest part of packaging is keeping the costs down, which is why many bakeries simply use plain white boxes and bags from warehouse stores or supply stores. This works fine if someone is coming into your physical bakery and purchasing a cookie to eat on the run, but what if they are buying a pie they want to take to a party? What if they are buying something online?

There are ways to keep costs down while standing out:

- Use labels. Labels can be designed once by your graphic designer and then printed out by you on your home computer. You can print them onto stickers and stick them on boxes or bags. A simple black and white label is an effective way to get your brand on your packaging.

◆ Consider buying in bulk. Many companies will give you a break on pricing if you buy a certain number of bags or boxes. You can do custom boxes this way at a lower price. Remember two things: You have to store them somewhere, and if something happens and you don't stay in business, you can't recoup that money.

◆ Consider one standout item, such as a certain color ribbon to tie bags shut or stickers to keep boxes closed.

◆ You can also offer beautiful packaging for a higher cost. While a lot of people may not pay for it, those giving gifts or who are taking something to a party may be willing to pay extra for packaging. You can easily find pretty packages in craft stores and discount stores that you can mark up to make a decent profit.

◆ Be creative. In some bakeries the packaging stands out more than the product. One bakery in my area sells cookies on an actual cookie sheet, and pies in beautiful ceramic pie plates. Another bakes chocolate cupcakes in small, unglazed flowerpots and then decorates them with flowers and such. How about putting peanut butter cookies in an empty and clean peanut butter jar with your label? You'll have to incorporate the cost of these add-ons into the prices, but many people will pay for creativity and something that no on else offers.

Overall packaging tips:

◆ First and foremost, you don't want your baked goods to get damaged. It's relatively easy to avoid when boxing up a pie, but sometimes hard to avoid when trying to make a dozen cookies fit into a box that doesn't quite work. While you want to save money, it's better to use two boxes for presentation.

◆ Choose packages that fit the item. Unless you only sell one item in one size, you'll probably have to get several types of packages in order to avoid having to cram something into a box or bag that doesn't fit. Not only will this cause your item to be damaged, but also it just looks unprofessional.

♦ Packaging items for shipping is different than packaging for local sale. You must use a sturdy container, it must be airtight and packed in tightly with no room for movement at all. Before you offer everything you have for shipment, you should consider that some things just do not ship well, such as items decorated with icing (unless you freeze them first). Ask at the post office or shipping carrier for tips about shipping food products. It's a good idea to test ship all of your products before offering them for sale online. A great way to find out how to ship is to place an order with an online competitor and see how it arrives to you.

♦ Make sure that if you sell items at local coffee shops, grocery stores or other wholesale outlets that your items are packaged individually and have a label that states the name of your bakery and website address.

♦ Don't try to simply package everything in one container. For example, packaging a soft and moist cookie with biscotti or another type of hard cookie can cause the hard cookie to become soft. This is especially important when shipping something in a container that is airtight.

If all else fails and you simply don't have time to worry about packaging right now, you should at the very least make sure that your items fit properly in the containers you choose, and that the overall look is appealing.

Now that you've got branding and creating your image down, we're going to take it up a notch and talk about getting customers, advertising and marketing. So if you're ready, let's move on to the next chapter!

Chapter 6

Promotion

If there's one thing any seasoned business owner will tell you, it's that it doesn't matter how great of a product you have, if people don't know you exist, you'll never sell anything.

In this chapter, we're going to go over the best ways to market your products, and get your name out there. Before you start panicking because you think it's going to cost you a bunch of money you don't have, relax; some of the best methods of marketing and advertising don't have to cost you anything. We're going to go over the best ways to market your products, and while some of them may cost a little bit of money, it's money well spent because without customers, you have no business. So grab your notebook and get ready to take some notes and jot down ideas. Creativity is key to an effective marketing plan, and you don't have to do what everyone else is doing to succeed.

What Are You Trying to Sell?

Before you can begin getting customers in the door, you have to ask yourself some questions. Of course, you know what you are selling, but why would your customers buy from you? What are you offering? If you offer an amazing product, you'll have no problem getting your customers to purchase your products, but the key is getting them to notice and taste your goods first, and this will be your biggest challenge, especially in the beginning. So figure out exactly who your customers are and what you can give them that no one else can. If you've followed the steps in this book, this shouldn't be too difficult, but it's very important right now when you need to bring in your customers.

Traditional Methods of Advertising

When you first think of advertising, what do you think of? Television commercials? Newspaper ads? Yellow Page ads? If you're new to business these things are probably the first things that pop into your mind, but there are reasons these may not work for you right away:

- ◆ They're expensive

- ◆ They require advanced planning

- ◆ They're not as directly targeted as other methods

- ◆ They can be out of date

Now, this doesn't mean they can't work for you down the road. These are very effective marketing tools; they're still used frequently, after all, but there are more modern and cost-effective marketing methods that may work better for you, so let's put these on the back burner for now.

Web Advertising

We talked a bit about the Internet in the last few chapters, so you should know by now how important it will be to your business, but now we're going to go over how you can use it to generate new customers and drive sales like never before. There are several methods of online advertising, and while the costs can vary greatly, it probably won't be nearly as expensive as you think. First though, let's look at the benefits of online marketing for your business:

- ◆ For most people, the Internet is part of their daily lives, and it's the first thing they look at in the morning and the last thing they look at before bed. It only makes sense that you want to be where people are looking. Think about how you search for a business. If you need a plumber for example, do you get out your trusty Yellow Pages and flip through the alphabetical listings until you find the term "plumber"? Probably not. If you're like most people, you head to the Internet and type "plumber" into a search engine. You may even type your city or zip code to get more targeted results. This is how people search for everything these days, from plumbers, to repair people, to yes, bakeries.

◆ Web advertising is easy to do. In most cases, if you want to place an ad on the Web, you don't even have to talk to someone; you can just create your ad, upload it and pay for it in a few minutes.

◆ It requires little planning. If you have a promotion idea today that you want to start in two days, you can sit down and send an email to your subscribers right now and they'll know about it in a few minutes. Some print publications need you to submit your ad weeks in advance, so they require a lot of planning.

Types of Online Advertising

There are many types of online advertising, and while some are better than others, you want to take advantage of as many as you can so that when someone types a keyword in a search engine, they have several listings for your business. Read on for the best online marketing methods.

Email Marketing

Email marketing is one of the most powerful advertising tools today. Everyone who uses the Web has email, and many people check it daily. You can send news about your business, coupons and more, and you hit everyone on your list in a matter of minutes.

Who Do You Send Emails To?

This is important. You only want to send emails to people who have specifically signed up for your mailing list. People take spam very seriously, and if too many people get emails from you that they don't remember signing up for, you'll get a bad reputation as someone who practices unsavory business tactics, and you could even get blocked from your Internet Service Provider as a spammer. It doesn't matter how great your product is, if people think you are unethical, they won't buy from you. So do not be tempted to send to random addresses, personal addresses, or to buy bulk email address lists from companies you find online. It will take time to collect a lot of email addresses, but you in the end, you will have a list of people who actually *want* your information instead of people who you don't know anything about.

How To Collect Email Addresses

There are several ways to collect email addresses legitimately, starting with your own website. You should have an easy way for users to sign up for your emails on your site. This can be in the form of a box where they simply enter their address and hit enter. When asking people to sign up, you should state two things very clearly:

- What they are signing up for. This can be just a brief sentence telling them they will receive news, coupons, discounts or whatever you plan on sending them.

- Your privacy policy regarding what you do with the information you collect. It doesn't have to be long, just has to state that you will not share or sell the information you collect.

When you sell at farmer's markets and other events, have a sheet where customers can sign up to be on your email list.

Should You Collect Other Information Besides Email Addresses?

Some sites collect full contact information in addition to email addresses, but this is really up to you. If you aren't going to send out mailers or call your customers, then you may not want to ask them for this information. Web users generally have a short attention span and may not like to share a lot of information. Asking them for too much may scare them off entirely.

Some Tips On Sending Emails:

◆ You have to find the right frequency to send out emails. Too many and they'll never get read, too few and users will forget about you. Remember, it's likely that your customers are receiving emails from many other companies, but they probably won't read them all.

◆ Make sure your emails have a purpose and that they contain information your customers want. Coupons and discounts are always good, exciting news such as new menu items is good; anything that is too long or not immediately useful will probably end up in the trash. Send too many things that people don't read and they're likely to unsubscribe or report you as spam.

◆ There are websites, such as mailchimp.com or aweber.com, that are excellent for email marketing. You can create and send targeted emails, create schedules and manage lists. They're not that expensive (Mail Chimp is free up to a certain number of users), and are a great way to keep everything under control.

Social Media

You may already use sites like Facebook and Twitter to share personal information and connect with friends, but did you know it can be an even more amazing tool for businesses to use to get in touch with customers?

Let's compare Facebook to an email marketing campaign. When you create a business page for Facebook, users can "add" or "like" your page. Every time you post a new item on your newsfeed, everyone on your list receives these updates in their newsfeed. Since many people check their Facebook page several times a day (many people check Facebook more than they do their email), they'll see your posts when they check their newsfeed. You're basically posting your information where people are looking, one of the biggest keys to successful advertising.

Social networking is also a great way to connect with your customers. It's easy for users to go to Facebook and post a question on your wall, or share a recent story or photograph about your business. If you use Twitter, users can retweet your news, effectively sharing your information with hundreds of other potential customers you may not be reaching otherwise.

In addition to Facebook and Twitter, there are plenty of other social networking sites:

- Sites like Foursquare and Gowalla allow users to check in at your business using a GPS-enabled mobile device. While you may not have a specific place of business, you can offer discounts and promotions for checking in at places where you are selling for the day, such as farmers markets, or craft fairs. For safety reasons, you should probably not ask users to check in at your home if that's where you will be doing pickups.

- Yelp is a review site where users can post reviews of restaurants and other businesses in the area. They create profiles, add friends, and make recommendations based on their preferences. You can encourage your customers to leave you a positive review if they have a good experience. Do not offer them anything for doing so however, and do not create fake reviews for your own business. Yelp has ways of monitoring these, and violating them could make you seem unethical.

Which Social Media Site Should You Use?

If you try to keep up with every single social media site out there, you'll never keep up. This can be especially overwhelming if you aren't tech friendly and have a hard time using these sites. It can be a challenge to learn and build a following on a new site, even for experienced users.

The best thing to do is to try to stick with the most popular ones to start, and adapt if something major happens and everyone is using a new site. For example, Facebook is huge right now, but Google+ is creeping up there. As of right now, not a lot of people are using Google+, so you can skip it, but do your best to keep up with what people are using. While MySpace was popular at one time, you probably wouldn't get a lot of benefit out of it today. There are other smaller sites that you can benefit from as well, but you'll probably have to pick and choose. A good way to handle it is to pick those you are comfortable with and stick to them, rotating as new ones become popular or others drop off the horizon. Then dedicate time each day or several times a week to update your social media. Once you get the hang of it, it won't take long.

There are all types of social media sites out there, most of which allow you to share music, videos or new stories. While there are some that are really popular, you should only focus on those that will help promote your business. Sharing news stories or funny pictures probably won't do much good, so signing up for a site like Reddit or Digg isn't necessary.

How Often Should You Update Your Social Media?

You have to find the right balance of posting your news, but it can be difficult. Post too much and you'll likely annoy people; if you don't post enough, your customers may forget about you.

The best way to go is to follow a few of your competitors and see what kind of information they post and how often. Don't copy them, but just seeing what they have to say, and others' reactions, can be a great inspiration when deciding on your own postings.

Remember, you only want to post relevant information that your customers will find useful. As long as you follow this rule, you'll be a social media queen in no time!

Tips to Use Social Media to Market Your Business

- Like email, you don't want to bombard your customers with information. If your customers see your business too much in their newsfeed, they are likely to take you off their list.

- Don't send out the same information through different channels. Many of your customers will likely sign up for emails, Facebook updates and other methods; they don't want to read the same thing over and over. Diversify a bit. You can even send out things that you think are interesting but don't necessarily have anything to do with your business. For example, you can tweet an article that talks about the benefits of buying from local businesses. It's relevant, users may retweet it, while also sharing your name with hundreds of others. When sending emails however, the information should be about your business exclusively.

- Offer customers something for adding you on sites like Facebook. For example, you can post on your own website that users who add you on Facebook will receive a free baked good at the next farmer's market. This accomplishes two things; it gets them to sign up for your updates and allows them to try your products.

- Follow up. When your customers ask questions, leave comments or otherwise engage in communication with you, and you should always follow up in a timely manner. Not doing so can leave users feeling like you don't care about your customers, meaning they are less likely to try to reach out again.

- Maintaining your social media advertising can take time. If you don't want to do your own social media campaigns, there are companies that can do it for you. Many web designers do it as well, so ask your designer if they offer the service and what they charge. It's not that difficult to do yourself once you get the hang of it, but only you can decide how much your time is worth.

Placing Ads Online

Everywhere you look online there are ads. Ads on websites, ads on videos; there are even ads on the sides of Facebook and other sites. These are easy to place on other sites, and can be cost effective and directly targeted.

The price you pay for the ads depends on where you put them, how big they are, and how long you want to leave them up. There are many types of ads out there, and some you pay for only when a user clicks on them. Some you simply pay a fee for the amount of time the ad is left up.

Whether these are worth it is up to you, if you see a website where you think your ads will work, simply email the site administrator and ask them about advertising. Many sites have a page that explains their advertising policies.

Daily Deal Sites

Sites like Groupon and Living Social are becoming popular with consumers everywhere, and for good reason. The way they work is simple. Each day these sites feature different businesses that are offering generous discounts for customers to use their products and services, usually around 50 percent off or more. The customer buys the coupon through the website, paying upfront. They then print out the coupon and use it at the place of business. On some sites, such as Groupon, a certain number of deals have to be purchased before the deal is on; on others, the number doesn't matter. These types of sites are great for consumers, but can be both positive and negative for business owners.

Pros:

- ◆ They send out daily emails to users in your city, so it's directly targeted marketing.

- ◆ They can get customers to try your products, which is half the battle.

- ◆ Even customers who don't buy your coupon may see your business name and remember it at a later date.

Cons:

- They can be expensive to use. Most deal sites want to offer at least 50 percent or more, but then they keep half the upfront payment, meaning that the business owner can lose up to 75 percent.

- You'll get a huge rush after the coupon hits the market, so you'll need to be prepared to handle all of the orders. Not being able to fill them all can lead to angry customers, so make sure you are prepared by having extra hands ready.

- Many business owners claim to actually lose money on the deal if they don't come up with the right deal.

Should you use these types of sites? Only you can answer that question. They are perfect for small businesses like you who are trying to get exposure, but if you don't handle it correctly, the whole campaign could backfire. Losing money isn't the worst thing in the world if it brings you repeat business, but you have to be able to afford it if that were to happen.

The best thing to do if you are interested in this type of advertising is to submit a request through the website of your choice. There are also a lot of these types of sites, and maybe even one specific to your city, so before immediately going with the big ones that may be more expensive, you can try a lesser known one first and see how it goes.

Blogging

Blogging can be a great tool for marketing your business, and keeping your customers up to date on what's going on with your bakery. It can be a great way to get in touch with your customers, and is a great creative outlet where you can display pictures of your products and services.

Tips for Blogging for Your Business:

- ◆ Use blogging as a way of communicating with customers, not advertising to them. You can write about whatever you want, but you should keep it relevant to your industry.

- ◆ Encourage reader feedback by asking them to answer questions in the comments. Encourage conversation, but make sure you are part of it as well.

- ◆ Post relevant content, and post it often. Remember, you want the content you put on your blog to be exclusive to your blog and not the same content you've already sent your customers through email/social media and more. In your posts, you should talk to your customers like you are having a conversation, not like every post is a press release.

- ◆ You don't just have to write to get your point across. You can also make videos that you can share on YouTube, and then link them to your blog. Your videos can include everything from giving your customers a sneak peek into how your products come to life, to tips and tricks you'd like to share. This gives you presence on another major site, and increases your visibility on the Web.

- ◆ Have a constant stream of ideas to post on your blog by jotting down ideas as you think of them.

- ◆ Your blog posts don't have to be long, but they have to be well written and relevant. If you don't have the time or skills to keep your blog updated, consider hiring someone who can or skipping it altogether. You don't want to do anything that may have a negative impact on your business.

Free Products and Samples

Giving away free products is a great way to get people to try what you are selling, and will likely lead to sales. There are many ways to do this, and while there are costs involved, it is usually worth it. Some tips:

- Have samples available at every event at which you're a vendor. Allowing customers to taste your products beforehand can lead to a sale, as well as prevent the negative reaction someone may have after they have paid for something they don't like.

- Consider setting up at a community event and giving away free products. This can be costly, but can be wildly effective.

- Offer people free products for doing something: Signing up for your email newsletter, following you on Facebook, or referring friends.

- Always bring products to parties and other social events you are attending. Make sure they have the same quality and visual appeal as those you would sell, and bring a stack of business cards to share.

- Offer free products to those in your community who can help you: journalists, other bloggers in your community, reporters and others.

- Once in awhile, bring boxes of pastries or desserts to local offices. This is especially good if you offer something many office workers may purchase themselves in the morning: doughnuts, scones or other breakfast items.

Word of Mouth

Word of Mouth is perhaps the best advertising method around, but it's not something that happens overnight and it's not something money can buy. You can take certain steps to facilitate and encourage it, but the best word of mouth happens because you offer customers something they feel is worth talking about.

What is Word of Mouth Advertising?

Word of mouth is essentially exactly what is sounds like: Customers come into your business and try your services, and feel it necessary to tell others about your business. While word of mouth is a great marketing method, it can be negative as well. Understanding why people talk about the businesses they frequent is the key to generating the best word of mouth advertising.

Think about all of the businesses you deal with on a daily basis. It's probably a lot when you consider grocery stores, banks, dry cleaners, retail stores or restaurants. You spend money at these businesses, but you probably don't even think about the experiences you have while there unless something out of the ordinary happens or the business offers a product or service that simply can't be found elsewhere (which is rare these days).

So what's a small business owner like you to do to get the best word of mouth advertising? Well the answer is quite simple: Give your customers an experience that stands out. Make only the best products you can, and offer customer service that can't be matched. Some tips:

- Visit a similar bakery in your area. Buy something and evaluate the experience. Is the product good? Was the person you dealt with friendly? Was the experience memorable? What would have made it better?

- Make a list of all of the experiences dealing with a business that you've told other people about. It may take some time, but go ahead and list as many as you can. When you're done, look at your list. If I had to guess, I'd say most of them are negative. This is because negative experiences tend to stand out more than positive ones. This means that in order to get people to talk about your business in a good way, you have to go out of your way to make a good impression.

- Sometimes a good impression will only happen after a customer has bought your products a few times. For this reason, consistency is key. If someone buys your products five times and you were friendly for three of the transactions, but for two you were having a bad day, they probably won't remember you. If, however, you were incredibly friendly every time, they are more likely to remember. Be consistent.

◆ Go out of your way for your customers, listen to what they are saying, and think of a way you can help them. For example, if you have a customer who mentions she is buying an item for her two children to share, offer to cut it in half for her. Or if someone buys a large amount of products, offer to help her take them to her car. Simple things like this are remembered. Not only is your customer likely to tell her friends about your bakery, but also they may be more willing to use you over someone else in the future.

◆ Talk to your customers. If they seem undecided about a particular item, ask them what they need it for and offer suggestions for what products may work better.

◆ Offer some small service that others don't, but that will make you stand out. It can be the ability to place an order by text message, or maybe even packaging and shipping your products if someone is buying a gift.

◆ Know your products, and be able to answer questions with confidence.

◆ Give your customer your full attention.

◆ Don't be afraid to edit your policies a bit if it will help a customer. For example, maybe you have a customer who needs an order tomorrow, but your policy is orders must be placed three days in advance. If you have time to make the order in that timeframe, why not do it? The customer will remember you, and she is more likely to tell her friends what you did. Be careful about utilizing this tactic too much, or it could backfire. Also, do not ever promise anything you can't deliver.

◆ Encourage customers to talk about you.

- Customer service matters, and to a lot of people it is more important than the products themselves. In a time when a lot of big-box businesses don't have the resources to provide excellent customer service, it can be refreshing to be treated like a business owner appreciates you. Remember this, and only hire people who understand this.

- The most important thing about word-of-mouth advertising is to stand out in a positive way.

Final Marketing Tips:

As you can see there are many ways to market your business, and the sky is the limit when coming up with a great advertising campaign. Be creative, and remember the following in order to come up with the best way to get people to buy your products:

- The best advertising campaigns are memorable. Just because someone else has not done it, doesn't mean it won't work. In fact, if it makes you stand out, it may just work better.

- Customers respond better to short messages rather than long drawn out sermons about how great your business is. Keep it short and to the point.

- Even the best advertising campaigns take time to work. It's not likely that your customers are going to see one ad either online or elsewhere and immediately contact you to place an order. The idea is to get your name out there so that when someone needs your services, you are the first business they think of.

- It's important to seriously think through every aspect of an ad campaign before putting it out to the public. One botched campaign can make it seem like you are unprofessional or that you don't know what you are doing.

Marketing is one of the most important aspects to any business, and you should not take it lightly. You should use as many methods as possible to get the word out, but most important, live up to your customers' expectations by offering the best products and the best service imaginable, and eventually you'll have plenty of customers.

Chapter 7

It's All About Balance

Many people start home-based businesses because they think that staying at home will allow them to spend as much time as possible with their families. While this is true to a point, once you get in the swing of things, you'll find out it's much different than you think.

In this chapter, we're going to go over how to balance everything. Don't think you need that? What are you going to do when you've got a huge order to get done and you've got a small child in the kitchen who desperately needs attention? It will happen, and it will be frustrating.

There are some things you need to remember before you get started or you'll find yourself in a mess of family members and customers that need your attention at the same time, leaving you to decide which is more important. You'll feel like everything is out of control, and you'll feel like you're not giving your family or your business the attention they need, yet you'll still find you have no free time.

Luckily, with some advance planning before you start, you can avoid most of that. Grab your trusty notebook. Read the following and make sure you understand it. Read it again if you have to; this is important stuff!

- ♦ First, you need to keep in mind that you are starting a business. Where you work isn't important and your customers won't care that you are overwhelmed. They are paying for a service, and expect it to be provided to them. If you don't go in expecting sympathy, you'll be in a much better position.

- Now, with that being said, you still have a family to think about. They are the most important part of your life, and probably a big reason you're doing this, right? While you can expect sympathy from them, you should not expect that they give up everything for your business.

- So, the first thing you'll need to do is to focus on keeping these two entities separate from each other. This will be difficult since you are basically setting up shop in your family's living area, but it has to be done. Don't worry. You can do it.

Start by sitting down with your family and talking to them about what to expect. This can be difficult at this point, since even you don't know exactly what to expect, but you need to discuss this with them. You should have already talked to them a little bit about the idea to make sure you have their support, but now you'll need that more than ever.

- First, make a list of what is important to you right now. Include everything in order of importance, and don't limit it to just people. It can include hobbies, or any activities you're involved in. Your list may look like this:

  - Spouse/Children

  - Outside family members (parents, siblings, etc.)

  - Friends

  - Playing/practicing piano

  - Afternoons at the park with a family pet

  - Volunteering at my child's school

◆ Make your list as long as you want, just try to keep it in order of importance. Once you have your list, look it over and decide what needs to stay and what needs to go. Obviously, you want to keep your family on the list, and probably your friends, but can you live without volunteering at your child's school? If so, maybe you should give that up for now. Also, keep in mind that you don't necessarily have to give up anything; if you can cut back on several things to make more time available, this can work too. Be realistic with this exercise. For example, if you have to significantly cut back your piano lessons and practice, are you really getting anything out of it? Maybe it would be easier to cut it out for now rather than have it play a role of obligation in your life.

◆ Also keep in mind that you don't have to give up anything for good. Ideally, once your business grows, you'll be able to hire employees to help so that you can enjoy the fruits of your hard work in the beginning.

◆ Next, you want to establish separate space for your business. This may be a little bit difficult since you will be spending much of your time in the kitchen, which is a family area, but you need to separate them as much as possible. Remember in the last chapter when you created a schedule? You need to stick to it as much as you can, and always keep your family posted on your schedule. In addition, you will need to do some office work, such as paying bills, taking orders, etc. You should have a small office or area set up where you can do those things.

◆ When you are scheduled to be working, make sure you are working. This is perhaps one of the hardest things that comes with working out of your house, but it's also one of the most important. Don't allow yourself to get sidetracked and get your work done. This way, you won't have to cut into family time for work related stuff. Make sure your family knows that when Mommy's working, she is not to be disturbed for anything other than an emergency. This will take some getting used to if you've always been available to your family at the drop of a hat, but it is necessary for true balance.

- Make sure that you schedule time family time, time for you and your spouse, and time for yourself. During these times, don't talk about your business; instead, focus on having fun and spending time together. Do everything you can to not allow business activities to overlap or cut out this time or your family will very soon feel neglected.

- Remember that other people live in the house too. When you're making out your schedule, try to think about what other people in the household may be doing. For example, you don't want to schedule a marathon baking session right through the dinner hour when everyone will be hungry and wanting to roam the kitchen. Instead consider doing that when your husband is at work and the kids are at school. Office time can be easier to schedule when others are in the house because you can just shut the door, or if you must have peace and quiet, you can head to the library or coffee shop for an hour or so.

- Manage interruptions, and there will be plenty. This goes both ways. Don't answer your business phone when you are with your family, and don't allow your kids to interrupt you while you are working.

Planning Your Schedule

One of the most important things about achieving balance is the ability to schedule everything just so, and then stick to the schedule. It can be hard, especially if you've been able to kind of go with the flow before now. But it must be done. Doing it before you get too frazzled will help prevent burnout in the future. So how do you plan a schedule that works for you and your family? Read on for an easy scheduling plan that anyone can do.

- First you'll need a way to easily change your schedule, while still being able to see at a glance what you've got going on. I recommend getting a big white board, or even chalkboard, that you can hang in your kitchen or other area that you'll see often. In fact, I would even get two, one for your weekly schedule and one for daily, but this may depend on how much room you have.

♦ In order to plan your schedule effectively, you'll need to have some set times to make a schedule. So you should start with a monthly calendar or planner. A calendar in your smartphone or computer would be perfect here. This is where you'll dump all items when you hear about them, no matter how far in advance. You'll have to get used to putting everything in this, so ideally you want something that you have with you all the time. If you use an electronic calendar, you can easily put repeating events in, so for example, if you bake every Monday from 9 a.m. to 3 p.m., you can put that in easily for every Monday.

♦ Next, you'll want to plan your schedule on a weekly basis. This is where your first whiteboard comes in. Each week, at the same time (such as Sunday night), you'll plan for the following week. Divide your whiteboard into seven sections, and write out what you've got going on according to your monthly calendar. List everything, whether business or personal. Once you get the hang of things, it shouldn't take you very long to simply lay out your week.

♦ Each night (or each morning), you want to make a detailed schedule for the next day. This is where you'll list everything you've got going on, and the time you want to do something. Your daily schedule may look something like this:

- 8 a.m. – Walk/exercise

- 9 a.m. – 3 p.m. Bake

- 3:15 p.m. – Pick kids up at school

- 4 p.m. – 5 p.m. – Answer business emails

- 6 p.m. – Dinner and family time

You want to include your kids' activities, social events and everything you have going on in your daily schedule. The whiteboard allows you to make changes as they come up (and they will).

I know it seems kind of daunting in itself to plan this every day, but once you get used to it, it will take a few minutes and you'll have a clear picture of your week and your day available at all times.

Tip: Of course it's important to stick to your schedule, but you should try to really stick to it as if you have someone waiting on you. In the example above, you're scheduled to bake at 9 a.m. after exercising, so you should do everything you can to finish, get showered and be in the kitchen ready to start at 9 a.m. on the dot in order to get everything done on time.

Setting Boundaries

Like we discussed previously, you can't do everything. So it's up to you to decide what to include and what you'll have to put aside for now, but one thing you must do when planning your schedule is to set boundaries and rules for yourself. These will differ with each person, but the goal is to clearly separate business from your family and personal life. Follow these tips for setting boundaries:

- Set an end to your workday. You can make it the same every day, or you can do it when you plan your daily schedule, but end it at a certain time, just as if you were going to work and getting off at a certain time.

- Many times people who work at home feel it's OK to combine things, such as your phone lines, to save money. Do NOT do this. You can easily add another line to your existing account for a few dollars a month, and you may be able to get a free phone. Use that number for all of your business calls, including the ones that come from customers to place orders. Set business hours, record those on the voicemail, and do not answer the phone outside of those hours. When you plan family time, it should be outside of those hours so that you aren't interrupted with business. Do not give anyone who is related to your business your personal phone number.

- Set up an email account strictly for business as well, and dedicate times to answer those emails, even if they are in 15-minute increments throughout your day. Because we're always connected to our email and social media accounts, we feel like we have to respond to everything immediately, but that's only the case if you allow it to be so. If you have a smartphone or tablet with email, I strongly recommend you do not put your business email account on it if you can't control the ability not to look at it. You should schedule time every day to answer emails so that they all get answered within 24 hours (except weekends), but do your very best to not worry about them outside of those timeframes.

A word about scheduling and boundaries:

In the beginning, business will be light, and you'll be tempted to stray from these rules, but resist the urge. Once you're busy, it can be hard to form good habits. Do it now, and if you have a little free time when you don't have any emails or the phone's not ringing, enjoy it while it lasts.

Keeping Up With Household Chores

You're going to find very quickly that when your house is also your place of business that things can get chaotic pretty quickly, and one of the first things to suffer will probably be household chores. There are several ways to combat this, but you'll have to be proactive.

- Make a list of what needs to be done and how often. You may be able to amend your current schedule a little to give yourself a break. For example, do your sheets really need to be changed once a week, or can it be stretched to once every two weeks? You'll have to make these decisions yourself.

- If your kids are old enough, they can help. Teenagers should be able to do their own laundry, and even small kids can help by putting their dishes in the dishwasher or feeding pets. This may be an adjustment, but you need to talk these things out with your family now, before your life gets on the crazier side.

- If your husband helps you with the household chores, that's great, let that continue. If he does not, then you need to help him understand that while you were able to do it before, you probably will not now. Don't try to push everything off on him; he's working too, but let him know that even though you will still be spending the majority of your time at home, you will be working and won't have time to do everything.

- If you are going to have customers come to your house for pickups, you need to make sure your house is presentable, at least in the areas that they will see. This includes the outside, as well as any areas they may see. Remember, they are eating what you are creating, so if they see a messy house, they may think twice about placing another order. Personally, I like the idea of setting up pickups at a location other than the house. Farmer's markets or other meeting places are ideal, but it is much easier to have pickup hours at the house since you can get other things done while you are waiting for customers. Just remember, if you owned a retail bakery, you would keep it clean and presentable; you should do the same at the house.

- Set a schedule for chores, and stick to it. Like every other aspect of a home-based business, getting sidetracked can have disastrous results. You'll probably find that if you focus, you can have all of your household chores done quickly and efficiently by penciling it in on your calendar for an hour or two each week.

- As far as keeping your kitchen clean, you're going to have to come up with a system. You don't want to have to clean up last night's dinner mess before you can get started working every day. It has to fit your family's habits, but if you are not already in the habit of cleaning your kitchen after every meal, you should be. Have family members bring all dishes to the kitchen when they are done (or now may be a good idea to institute the rule that eating is at the dining room table only), and keep everything as clean as possible.

- When working in the kitchen, get in the habit of cleaning as you go, and try not to allow yourself to stand around while your cupcakes are baking; there's always something that can be done. Try to keep as busy as possible.

How involved with your family be in your business?

In the beginning, you should be able to count on your family to help you out, but how involved do you really want them to be?

The answer to this will vary depending on several factors. While you may be expecting support from your husband, if he has a job of his own, he may not be able to devote time to your business.

If your kids are older, you can expect some help, but try to remember that there's a fine line between help and a part-time job. Your family will soon resent your new business if they find themselves working while not getting paid. If you have the money, you can offer your teenagers an hourly wage for helping, but this is up to you.

In the beginning, you'll find yourself needing help, and maybe even thinking about paying someone minimum wage to have an extra pair of hands around. Money issues aside, you need to think carefully who you choose. Often the first place we look is family members and close friends. Maybe your sister is a stay-at-home mom and can help you out during the day, or you think you'll be able to see your best friend more often if she helps you a couple nights a week. There are a couple problems with this line of thinking, although every small business owner tends to go down this path at one point. Consider that:

- Having coffee and a conversation or a fun night out is much different than working with someone.

- Friends or relatives won't take the job as seriously working for you as they would someone else, and a stranger will be more likely to work harder for you than a family member. You may think this isn't true of your friends and family, but it probably is. It's human nature.

- It will be much harder for you to get your work done if you have someone close to you around. Gossip, chitchat and goofing off can seriously derail productivity. It's better to work hard by yourself than not get as much done and still have to pay an employee.

- Working too closely with family members can have a damaging effect on the relationship. Remember, you have to be the boss. This is a hard position for anyone in any situation, but are you going to fire your sister for showing up late or ruining yet another batch of cookies due to carelessness? Probably not.

While it can be the easiest way to find employees, I'm going to vote strongly against hiring close family members for your business. You're going to have enough stress as it is, you don't need to put a rift in your family because someone is not working out. You know how families are; get mad at your sister and suddenly your mom's not speaking to you and family functions become unbearable. Don't do it. You can thank me later.

Finding Free or Affordable Help

Aside from your family, there are ways you can get help with your business, and they are surprisingly affordable.

- Consider what you can barter. Maybe the mom down the street will be glad to help you out for a few hours here and there if you'll agree to make her kids birthday cakes. Or maybe you can send your kids to friends' houses when you're busy in exchange for watching their kids when you're not. Be creative, make offers, and see what you can find.

- Consider an intern of sorts. Many culinary students – or other people who want to get in the baking business – would love to help out in order to learn how things are done. In exchange for teaching them the business, you'll get an extra pair of hands once in awhile. You don't have to limit yourself to just one, just make sure they're truly getting something out of the deal.

◆ Teenagers can be excellent help and will work for minimum wage, especially if you have specific tasks for them to do, such as spending two hours icing cookies or other tedious tasks you don't have time for.

◆ Many businesses try to find seasonal help around the holidays when they know they will be bringing in extra income. You can too, just be clear about whether or not you will be able to hire them after the holidays. Many people take seasonal jobs in the hopes of getting hired on afterwards; if you know you absolutely cannot do it, make sure you are clear about the end date.

◆ Consider contract employees. This can be a perfect solution when you have a large order you need to get done. With a contractor, you can hire someone for a specific job, or just one or two days, and you can pay them a flat rate. They'll have to pay their own taxes, and you don't have to worry about keeping an employee on when you no longer need them. Just make sure you are upfront about what you're offering; even contract employees can expect regular work, but let them know that if it works out you will be happy to call them in the future.

It's important to remember to never take advantage of people. Ask yourself if they are truly getting a fair deal, especially in the case of interns or trades. You'll likely need help frequently as business picks up, and it can be nice to have people on hand who are glad to help. Offering everyone who helps you the benefit of free products, even if it's just extras at the end of the day, can be a great perk too. Also, NEVER promise to pay people if you just can't afford it. This can lead to people badmouthing you in the community, or even lawsuits. Unless you are willing to pay out of your own pocket regardless of how business turns out, you'll have to find a way to do it yourself.

What about small children?

While your life will change drastically going from stay-at-home mom to businesswoman, it will not change as much as it will for your children, especially if they are too young to really understand why you are doing this. Read on for ideas on how to make this transition easier for them while still devoting the necessary amount of time to your business.

- Try to keep as much the same as you possibly can. For example, if you take your kids to school in the morning and tuck them in at night, try to continue to do that. One of the best benefits of owning your own business is making your own schedule; you should do so in a way that benefits everyone, not just you.

- If your kids are still young enough to need full-time attention or they simply can't help but bother you during your working hours, you should consider hiring outside care or seeking help from a friend or family member. It may seem silly to send your kids to a babysitter while you stay in your own home, but if you are trying to bake and have a toddler constantly pulling on your arm, neither of you is benefitting from the situation. You don't have to send them to full-time daycare; maybe you can send them to Grandma's for a couple hours a day or several times a week. The kids will benefit because they'll get the attention and care they need, and you can focus on your business.

- While it may not be ideal, you can schedule to work after your kids have gone to bed, even if it's just for an hour or two. You will get the most work done if it is uninterrupted, so you'll have to take it while you can get it.

- If your kids must be there during your working hours, you can try to let them help. Small kids love working in the kitchen with mom. A few things to consider with this approach: You don't want kids working with items you are going to sell, so maybe try setting them up with their own small table and scraps of pie dough that they can make their own creations out of. You also want to make certain that they are not wandering around the kitchen where they can get burned by a hot pan or otherwise injured. If you can make it work, this can be a great solution to kids who have a hard time adjusting to less time with mom; they'll feel like they are spending time with you and doing something fun to boot.

My husband feels neglected. Now what?

Even if you've discussed this with your husband before you started and he was onboard, the reality is that once you start your business, there is a major adjustment period, especially in the beginning when you'll feel like you have to devote all of your time in your business. Some tips for keeping your husband happy:

- While you may list your husband and your kids on the same line on the priority list, the reality is that your children's needs will probably get taken care of first; this is only natural, and expected. Try your best to realize this and devote extra time with your husband, even if it's just watching a movie together after the kids have gone to bed.

- Talk about everything. Even if this is your business and you are doing it all on your own, you should still talk to your husband about major decisions and keep him in the loop. Remind him that you are doing it for not just you, but also the entire family, and he will benefit someday too.

- Ask for his advice, and listen to him. He'll feel like he has more of an input than if you are just on autopilot all the time.

- Take some time, even if it is just one night a month that is dedicated only to your husband. Get dressed up, go to a nice restaurant and spend time talking the way you did before life got in the way. Put this on the schedule and stick to it.

- Do everything you can to avoid mixing your family and business life. I know it's been said over and over in this chapter, but it is worth repeating, as this is the most important aspect to achieving the perfect home/work balance.

True Life/Work Balance

After you've read this chapter, you should have a clear idea of your priorities, and how you're going to hang on to the things that are important to you. It will take time to get your schedule right, and get the perfect balance between everything you are trying to handle. You'll step on some land mines along the way, but as long as you have a picture in your head of what is important and why you are doing everything you are doing, you can work out your issues along the way.

While balance is important, nothing is as important as taking time for yourself, which is what the next chapter is all about.

Chapter 8

Taking Care of Your Mind, Body and Spirit While Balancing it All

By now you should have the basics of the business down, and you're probably ready to be the top home baker in your area, which is great! It's a great feeling to be good at something, and to have people you don't know rave about your product is a feeling you can't get from anything else. You can only go up from here!

Not so fast. Unfortunately, great success comes at a price, and for small business owners everywhere, that price can be high stress, an unbalanced lifestyle, and quite possibly, your sanity. You will feel like you have to put your all into your business, and in the beginning it will be a sacrifice you have to make to get where you need to be. You'll have to neglect your family, your friends and your personal life, and that's OK, but only for a while. You have to have an end date as to when the madness will be done and when your life will be normal again.

With those things being said, you will still have to make sacrifices, and you'll have to make choices you don't like. The business will be an important responsibility and will take up a good portion of your life. The key is to not let it consume your whole life, but if you don't get it under control now, you'll struggle with it throughout your career.

So where to begin? Well, we went over many of these things in the last chapter, so if you didn't read through that one thoroughly, you should go back. To sum it up, it's about making priorities, and separating your business and personal lives so that everyone gets their fair share of your time and energy.

We went over how to provide your family and friends with the time they need from you, but we left out the person who needs you the most: You. You deserve an entire chapter, and that's what this one is for.

Failing to take care of yourself is the easiest way to lose control of everything in your life, and doing so can cost you your family, your friends and your business.

Time For Yourself

You are going to find yourself juggling many hats in the beginning of your home bakery career. After you've taken care of the business, your children, husband and house, it will seem like there is nothing left for you.

You can't let this happen. It will be difficult, but you have to fit in time for yourself or you will quickly burn out. It doesn't have to be big gaps of time; rarely will you get an entire day to yourself, but you must do it. Follow these tips for avoiding stress and taking time for yourself:

- ◆ Schedule it. Yes, this will probably be your new motto when it comes to time management, but this is the only way you will get things done. Get a calendar or planner with timed slots and schedule your time down to the minute.

- ◆ Take small time slots if that's all that's available. Taking a 15-minute walk after you drop your kids off at school before you start working every day can save your sanity.

- ◆ Don't confuse time by yourself working as time for yourself. Your time for yourself should be spent doing something you enjoy;

browsing a bookstore, taking a bubble bath, or walking the dog are examples of ways to get your "me time" in; sitting at a desk answering emails about your business is not.

While this covers the basics, there's much more to it than that, which is why we've created a list of rules that will help you keep yourself in check, and make yourself a priority.

Rule No. 1: Put Yourself First

This is probably the most difficult task you will face; particularly because you are probably used to worrying that everyone else's needs get taken care of. You start with your kids because they need you the most, and after they get their time in, the little bit left goes to your husband, your mother, your friends and anyone else who demands a piece of your time. After that, you have so little time, that the five minutes you get to spend in the shower each morning becomes the highlight of your day.

The truth is that no one benefits from you if you're a frazzled, stressed-out mess, including you. So we've created this list to help you, *and* those you love, get the most out of you and your awesomeness.

Putting yourself first doesn't have to mean neglecting everyone else. All it means is that you have to make yourself a priority. Which brings us to the next rule.

Rule No. 2: Learn to Say No

Admit it. You've done things that you didn't want to. If you're being totally honest, that list is way longer than you'd like. Everyone does it, some more than others.

Why Do We Do It?

It goes back to what we said in Rule No. 1. You put everyone's needs before yours, mixed with a little bit of wanting to please everyone all the time. You've probably learned that you can't please everyone all the time, yet you to continue to do things you don't want to. It's OK. You're not alone. Everyone does it to some extent, but if you're going to achieve true balance, you need to learn to stop.

Easier said than done. Unfortunately, you will have to do things you don't like, but the key is determining which things are necessary and which you can skip without guilt. The next time you are asked to do something by someone else — anything — ask yourself the following questions:

1. Is it necessary? (An emergency, a business obligation, some family events, things relating to your children)

2. Will it benefit you in some way?

3. What will happen if you say no?

4. Do you want to do it?

5. Will you have to rearrange your schedule?

6. Does the asker want you to repay a favor?

7. Will it set you behind in some way?

For example, let's use a casual friend inviting you to a girl's night out on a Friday night two weeks from now. Normally, you may say, "I'll be there" without a thought, but answering these questions you get:

1. No

2. If you need a fun night out, then yes, but if you don't want to go, it won't.

3. Your friend may nag you a bit, but ultimately, nothing.

4. That's up to you, but if you truly don't want to go, you should not.

5. If you have something else planned, such as movie night with your children or date night with your husband, you should say no.

6. Probably not.

7. Probably not, but maybe.

In some cases, the answer is easy, such as in the example above, or if someone asks to do something you don't want to do and you have no reason to do it. Question No. 5 is important because unless it is an emergency situation, you should not reschedule family events, or anything that will put you behind.

One tip: You don't have to make up excuses why you can't do something. You can tell truth to the best of your ability. If you're busy, it's easy. But if you just need a relaxing night at home, you should say it, and don't feel guilty about it. You may not want to come out and say you just don't want to do something, but you don't have to lie. These things have a way of coming out anyway.

Rule No. 3: Get Enough Sleep

Sleep is often one of the first places that we cut out when our schedule is overloaded because it's the easiest, but you shouldn't do it, and here's why:

◆ It's bad for your health. Numerous studies have shown that lack of sleep can cause weight gain, stress, and a host of other health problems. Going to bed late once in awhile is OK; doing son on a regular basis can have adverse reactions to your health.

◆ When you're tired, you move slower, you think slower and you are more likely to make mistakes. You're also not focused on the task at hand, which means it will take you longer to do a less effective job.

◆ You'll be in a better mood. Not enough sleep causes depression, moodiness and irritability.

Have trouble sleeping? Try these tips:

◆ Go to bed at the same time every night, and get up at the same time. Every night, even weekends.

- ◆ Avoid pills and other chemicals that help you sleep. They can be addicting, and you'll wake up groggy.

- ◆ Avoid sensory overload an hour before bed. Read instead of watch TV, and have decaf tea instead of soda or alcohol.

- ◆ Make sure your sleep environment is comfortable, including bedding and mattresses, temperature and lighting.

- ◆ Shoot for seven to nine hours a night, and don't sleep too much either.

It's very important that you schedule your day so that you can get everything in that you need to without cutting into your sleep. This can be difficult since we are trained from a young age to cut back on sleep when we need more time, but your body needs to rest in order to be its best. Oh, and FYI: You can't get caught up on sleep you've missed, so get out of the habit of saying "I'll make up my missed sleep this weekend".

Rule No. 4: Banish Time-Wasters

While having time to yourself is not in any way a time-waster, there are certain things that you can live without and you know what they are. Things like playing games on Facebook, watching YouTube videos, or anything else that you plan on only doing for a few minutes but that easily turn into hours before you know it.

It's different for everyone, and only you can determine what your time-wasters are, but if you can't limit them, you need to have the willpower not to do them. These seemingly harmless things will eat up your day faster than anything else you do, guaranteed.

To figure out what your downfalls are, try to monitor what you're doing throughout the day. If your problem is that you can't sit in front of your computer without browsing useless stories on the Web, try setting a timer. Work on the task at hand for a solid 25 minutes and take a five-minute break. Do this until you get your work done. The key to this strategy is actually working for the full 25 minutes (no checking email, browsing photos, etc.) and forcing yourself to go back to work after the five minutes is up. This strategy helps many people and doesn't have to be used solely on the computer. All you need is a timer and you can use this trick anywhere: in the kitchen, while paying bills, or whatever it is you have to do.

You should also be aware of another major time-waster that is especially troublesome to those who work at home: talking on the phone. Since you work for yourself, if the phone rings and it's your best friend who wants to chat, or your sister wanting to vent about your mom, you may want to answer, but the problem is (and you can probably see where I'm going with this) these conversations can easily last hours. To combat wasting time on the phone, only answer when it's an emergency or someone you know will only keep you for a minute. For others, you can call them back when you have free time, or send a quick text saying you're in the middle of something and you'll chat later.

Rule No. 5: Find a Healthy Stress Reliever

No matter how balanced your life is, you will be stressed. It's unavoidable as a mom, wife and business owner. The key is managing it before it becomes a problem.

Some tips for managing stress:

- Deal with problems immediately. Letting them build will only push you to the point where you break.

- Talk about it. Whether with a trusted friend, your husband or a family member, sometimes seeing another point of view can be a huge relief.

- If you feel ready to explode for whatever reason, simply take a deep breath, count to 10 and walk out of the room. It may seem rude at the time, but it's much better than blowing up. After you've calmed down, go back and try to talk calmly about the problem.

- One of the biggest reasons we become stressed is because we take on too much without taking a break. So manage your schedule, and take regularly breaks.

It's important to find a few ways to relieve stress that aren't going to harm your bottom line. Unhealthy stress relievers include:

- Binging on junk food or other unhealthy foods like ice cream, cookies or cake

- Shopping and spending money you don't have

- Drinking excessively

- Smoking

- Recreational drug use

- Gambling

- Anything that is harmful to your well-being

That being said, there are a lot of healthy stress relievers. If you feel overwhelmed, take 15 minutes and try one of these:

- Have a cup of tea and read a book or magazine to take your mind off your problems

- Take a brisk walk

- Take your children outside and play, or play a board game

- Play with your pets

- Meditate

- Do some quick yoga poses

◆ Call a friend who will make you laugh, but don't talk about the issue of your stress

◆ Put on some headphones and listen to your favorite tunes to zone out for a few minutes

◆ Pray, or if you don't pray, simply sit and collect your thoughts until you feel better. This can work wonders on your soul.

◆ Write it down. If you have a journal, write down your thoughts and feelings. Fast and furiously, or slow and lazy, just get them out there. No journal? That's OK. The simple act of writing down your thoughts on a piece of scratch paper can be therapeutic. Even if you ball up the piece of paper and throw it away, you'll still feel much better.

While these are all great instant stress relievers, doing these activities even when not actively stressed can reduce stress levels overall.

Rule No. 6: Eat a Healthy Diet and Exercise on a Regular Basis

No two things will keep you quite as healthy as a healthy diet and regular exercise. Of course like everything else, these can be difficult to follow through with, but it can be done with a little willpower. The benefits are rewarding: you'll feel great, have more energy and be much more focused, and in addition, you'll be warding off disease and will keep the doctor at bay. If you don't take care of yourself, no one will.

Dieting tips:

◆ Focus on whole health foods and try to eat a wide variety of fresh fruits and vegetables.

◆ Avoid junk food and fast food.

- If you can't help eating leftover baked goods, find a way to deal with them quickly such as donating or giving them away rather than letting them sit and wait for you to eat them.

Exercise tips:

- Put exercise on your schedule, and then stick to it.

- You don't have to join an expensive gym to get a workout in, you can use DVDs walk or run outside, or invest in a piece of exercise equipment.

- Be unconventional. Running and playing with your dog for 20 minutes is great exercise, as is playing a sport with your kids.

- Yoga, Pilates, and weight lifting are all low-impact, relaxing ways to stay in shape.

- Partner with a friend. This is a great way to honor commitments and have fun at the same time.

Bottom line: You must take care of yourself if you want to lead a healthy balanced lifestyle, and nothing will help that as much as a healthy diet and exercise.

Rule No. 7: Take Care of Yourself

In addition to eating well and exercising, taking care of yourself can go a long way to your well-being, but it can be hard to come back after you've let yourself go.

While many of these rules involve taking care of yourself (such as getting enough sleep), there are other minor, yet important things you can do to keep your mind and soul healthy, such as:

- Get your hair done on a regular basis. It may seem trivial and you may think you don't have time to do it, but there's nothing quite like stepping out of the salon with a new cut and color. It's also a great way to get time for you.

♦ Buy yourself something nice once in a while. You don't have to spend a fortune, and you certainly shouldn't spend money you don't have, but buying yourself a small item says you care about yourself.

♦ Visit your doctor and your dentist on a regular basis, even if there's nothing wrong. Staying healthy is important to get everything you need done and still feel great about yourself.

♦ Get a massage once in awhile. It's relaxing, rejuvenating and will make you feel like you can conquer the world.

Rule No. 8: Tone Down Technology

Yes, technology is great, and you would not be able to start a thriving business from home without it. Not to mention all the cool things you can do these days, such as taking and sending instant photographs through text messages and always being connected to your loved ones.

So why should you tone it down? Because it probably drags you down sometimes and you don't even know it. Think about it. How often do you find yourself playing games on your computer for hours on end? Do you feel like you just have to answer the phone because you have it? Well, the truth is, you don't, and your body and brain can benefit from a little break now and then. I'm not suggesting getting rid of your cell phone, or not texting, but it really is not necessary all the time. Once you give it a short rest, you'll see that you feel more alive and focused.

Some tips on toning down technology:

♦ Live in the moment. Instead of posting on Facebook about the beautiful day, actually go outside and enjoy it. Don't tweet about how great your kids are; actually spend time with them and soak up that greatness.

- Make it a rule that you do not use your phone when you are in the presence of another person, whether your friend, spouse or even a cashier. It's rude, and you miss out on important things people may have to say.

- Make it a rule that everyone in the family leave their phone behind when coming to dinner, enjoying a meal in a restaurant or spending time together.

- Put your phone away or turn it off when you're doing another activity, even if it's just watching television.

- Designate certain times to be technology-free. It can be an hour a day, or a full day a week if you think you can do it. Your mind and spirit will thank you.

- Try to spend the last half an hour before bed free of all technology and electronics items: cell phone, iPod, computer and yes, television. You'll sleep better, and you really won't miss it. Get in the habit, and it will be one you don't want to give up.

You don't have to give up technology in order to be happy, but you may be surprised at how few things you miss when you give up your cell phone or your computer. If you're panicking at the mere thought of it: Stop. You can do it.

Rule No. 9: Focus

Focus. On what, you ask? Everything. No matter what you are doing, whether work or play, you will get significantly much more done if you just pay attention to what you are doing. This means no checking your email all day long if you're supposed to be working, no talking on the phone while you're baking, and no texting while playing with the kids, having coffee with a friend or worse, driving.

We've become a society of multitaskers, but the truth is, what is supposed to make us more productive actually makes us less. There are several reasons for this, starting with the fact that when you concentrate on more than one thing at a time, something always gets left out, leading to more work later on fixing things. Another reason not to multitask? It's hard to become an expert or even remotely good at something if you're doing everything halfway.

So stop trying to do more than one thing at a time, and focus. Some tips:

- Schedule everything, even breaks, and even time-wasters if you can't get rid of them completely.

- Stick to said schedule.

- Don't take your mind off something for a minute, such as reading a quick email, or answering the phone. This makes your brain change subjects, and it can be hard to get back on track.

- Keep a small notepad with you and if you think of something that needs done, write it down instead of switching gears. You can then look at your notes during a break and fit those things into your schedule accordingly.

- Set timers for everything, even if they're only for items that take a few minutes. Tricking yourself into thinking you have to get a certain task finished in a certain amount of time can make you focus on the task at hand. As an added bonus, you'll work faster.

If you've ever had days where you don't feel like you accomplished anything and can't figure out why, it was more than likely a lack of focus. Spend a few days tracking yourself and your habits, and you'll likely find that when your mind wanders, so does your productivity.

Rule No. 10: Ask For Help

There are many things you'll be able to get done on your own, and if you can, you should. However, sometimes things come up and you may need help. Ask for it. Don't be afraid to ask your husband, teenage children, friends and family members for help in a pinch. You may be surprised to find that many people actually want to help you, and are happy to do it. Don't forget to repay the favor, and do not overextend yourself.

Some tips:

- If you need to get out of the house, ask a neighbor to come over for a half hour and stay with the kids while you run to the local coffee shop and sit for a few minutes to collect your thoughts.

- Is business so good it's overwhelming? It's OK to ask your husband or even a close friend to pitch in and help you catch up, although you don't want to take advantage of anyone.

- If someone goes out of their way to help you out, show appreciation with a thank you card and some baked goods or a gift certificate.

Rule No. 11: Know When To Let Go

This is an important rule, and one that you should fall back on whenever you get super stressed. It goes hand and hand with "you can't do everything," "you can't please everyone," and "pick your battles."

The bottom line is that there comes a point when you're going to have to pick and choose what's important to you, and give up things that you may not want to.

You Can't Do Everything

Think about it: You're a mom, a wife, a friend, and now you want to add business owner to the mix. You can have all of these things, but you may not be able to also be in charge of the PTA, or continue with your twice-weekly Bible Study. The point is, you have to constantly evaluate your priorities and add or take things off your list. If you don't truly enjoy everything on your list, it may be time to let go. A good rule of thumb before automatically taking on a new activity is to ask yourself what you want to give up. If there isn't anything, then maybe now isn't the time to start something new.

You Can't Please Everyone

You probably know this is true, yet you try anyway. Well, it's time to stop. Make those who are truly important to you a priority, and do what you can for the rest. If you do something wrong, apologize, try to make it up to the person, but if that doesn't work, it's time to move on. Do not waste time on drama, pettiness and childish behavior. That's what your children are for.

Pick Your Battles

Think about the last time you were angry. What was it about? Was it something major, such as a betrayal by a loved one? Or was it something minor, like a bank fee you feel was unjust? Either way, sometimes, you just have to realize that you can't win every fight. I know, you don't want to give up, but is it really worth a few hours out of your day to try to get rid of a bank fee that's only a couple dollars? Stop saying "It's the principle," take a deep breath, and let it go.

The Result

If you've learned anything from the last two chapters, I hope it's that you can live the life you've always wanted, but not if you're a stressed-out, overwhelmed, unhealthy, frazzled mess.

Neglecting yourself is a surefire way to end up tired, sick, and useless to everyone in your life, which is the exact opposite of the life you want to live, right?

So, while it will be hard, make the changes you need to make NOW before your business is booming and you don't have time to think straight. Do it for your children, do it for your family, but most important, do it for you!

Conclusion

So by now, you should have a good grasp on what it takes to become a small business owner. It's not an easy journey, and there will be stressful times ahead, but if you take the time to think things through, you can have a rewarding career that you love, but that also gives you the flexibility and control to spend time with your family, your friends and your loved ones. Isn't that what life is about after all?

If you've learned anything by reading this book, I hope you came away with a sense of empowerment. I hope that as you were reading, you found yourself saying things such as "That doesn't sound so bad!" or "I can do this," because you know what? It's not, and you can.

Of course, you'll run across some things that you don't want to do. Who wants to figure out all that tax information, after all? But the truth is, for every great thing in life, comes pitfalls and sacrifices, and parts of it that you'd rather leave out. This includes even the things you love the most. You've changed many a diaper in your life, and you would do it again and again for the same rewards, wouldn't you?

That's what you can expect out of your business. A long, rewarding career, with a couple dirty diapers along the way. Some may be really dirty, but it won't be anything you can't clean up. You'll have to give it your all, and you'll have to make some sacrifices along the way. You'll feel burnt out, and stressed, and there will probably be a few times where you'll wonder why you thought this was a good idea in the first place. That's okay. Simply take a deep breath and go back and read the last chapter of the book.

You can use this book as a reference, and come back to it as often as you need to. Of course, everything isn't in here; there are some things you'll just have to learn as you go, but hopefully, once you've gotten in the swing of things, you'll be able to minimize surprises and enjoy your rewarding career as a small business owner.

Assuming you haven't actually gotten started with your plans, you should be pleased to know that when you go the next page, we've compiled a checklist of what you need to do, in order to get your business going. Don't forget to schedule a few breaks along the way, and of course, don't forget to take time for yourself. You're worth it!

Appendix

Checklist

You can use this list to walk through each chapter's steps. If you need more information on a particular item, you can look back through the book for details.

Getting Started (Chapter 1):

- Determine What You're Going to Sell

- Define Your Products

- Test Your Recipes

- Brainstorm Packaging Ideas

Getting Your Business Set Up (Chapter 2):

- Create Your Vision

- Create a Business Plan

- Research Your Local Health Regulations, Contact Health Department

- Organize Your Kitchen

- Begin Planning Your Schedule

Product Creation (Chapter 3):

+ Set Your Policies and Procedures

+ Perfect Your Recipes

+ Create a Production Schedule

Sales (Chapter 4):

+ Determine Where You'll Sell Your Products

+ Research Farmer's Markets and Craft Fairs Online

+ Begin the Process for Setting Up Your Own Website

+ Decide Whether You Are Going to Sell on Your Site/Third Party Sites

+ Contact Local Grocers, Restaurants and Coffee Shops

Creating Your Brand (Chapter 5):

+ Decide What Type Of Public Image You Want to Have

+ Create a Logo/Contact A Designer

+ Choose a Web Domain

+ Finish Your Website Creation

+ Talk to Your Web Designer About Getting Traffic

+ Finalize Packaging, Including Getting Labels, etc.

Promotion/Marketing (Chapter 7):

+ Determine Which Methods of Advertising You Will Use

+ Sign Up For An Email Marketing Service, Such as Aweber or Mail Chimp

+ Sign Up For Social Media Sites You Will Use

CPSIA information can be obtained
at www.ICGtesting.com
Printed in the USA
BVHW031818120920
588618BV00006B/291